SMOKEY

SMOKEY

Inside My Life

BY

Smokey Robinson

WITH DAVID RITZ

McGRAW-HILL PUBLISHING COMPANY

New York   St. Louis   San Francisco   Auckland   Bogotá   Hamburg
London   Madrid   Mexico   Milan   Montreal   New Delhi   Panama
Paris   São Paulo   Singapore   Sydney   Tokyo   Toronto

1 2 3 4 5 6 7 8 9 DOC DOC 8 9 2 1 0 9 8

ISBN 0-07-053209-5

Library of Congress Cataloging-in-Publication Data

Robinson, Smokey, 1940–
   Smokey : the soul of Motown / by Smokey Robinson.
     p. cm.
   Includes index.
   ISBN 0-07-053209-5
   1. Robinson, Smokey, 1940–   . 2. Soul musicians—United States—
Biography. I. Title.
ML420.R74A3 1988
784.5'5'00924—dc19
[e]   88-31183
                                        CIP
                                       MN

Book design by Eve Kirch

For our children:
Berry, Tamla and Trey Robinson
Jessica and Alison Ritz

Thanks to Gladys Justin Carr, vice president and publisher of McGraw-Hill's General Books Division, who made the marriage between Robinson and Ritz.

We also extend gratitude to Mike Roshkind, Aaron Priest, Tom Miller, Sherry Robb, Rose Ella Jones, Geraldine Burston, Sharon Burston, Steve Ivory, Roberta Ritz and Ray Baradat, soul researcher extraordinaire.

CONTENTS

Part Three—Agonies and Ecstasies

Part Four—Solo

Contents

Part Five—Up

The Storyteller

Smokey Robinson looks directly at you; his sea-green eyes are riveting. His soft speaking voice, like his singing voice, is high-pitched, honey-dipped, sweetly seductive.

Riding the band bus, in planes and limos and golf carts, talking till dawn in hotel suites, he tells you the story of his life with sadness, joy and wonder. He's enthusiastic and animated. He'll leap up and testify; he'll fall down laughing. He's straight-ahead, street, sincere. His luminous eyes are so startlingly clear, you suspect that, peering into them, you might see through to his soul. His curly hair bears traces of the blond coloring of his childhood. His skin glows with the tint of rich red clay. He's broad-shouldered and tall, his hands large, his waist trim.

Listening to him is effortless. His speech is fluent, his stories flow smoothly. He likes entertaining, likes making you laugh, likes to surprise.

He starts off with the most shocking story of all.
Listen.

The End

I was dying.

Four times during the night I'd wake up shivering, soaking wet, as though someone had thrown a bucket of water over me. Only it wasn't water; it was my own sweat.

Heart palpitations filled me with fear. My heart hammered so hard, I thought it'd explode out of my chest. For two or three beats my heart would seem to stop, pushing me to panic.

And then there was this pus, thick poisonous pus. Defecating, I was passing pus out of my body.

I had no stomach lining left. I had no hope. I heard things that weren't there; I saw things that weren't there.

I wouldn't go to the doctor 'cause I knew I had only a few months to live. I didn't need no doctor to tell me that.

I wouldn't ask friends for help because I wouldn't admit I needed any. But deep down, I knew. The Epidemic of the Eighties had caught up with me:

It was rock cocaine; rock cocaine was killing me.

It wasn't possible. It couldn't be me. I'd been a high school athlete. At seventeen, when the cats would ask me to smoke weed, I'd say, "No way. Y'all get that stuff outta my face."

True, I'd started smoking later on, after the Miracles made our first record, but I always had the shit under control. Could and would stop for months at a time. Nothing got in the way of my golf games or long-distance runs. Weed was no big deal. Just a little natural herb putting a funny filter over things. Nothing heavy.

Must have been in the late sixties when I saw cocaine for the first time. I refused to snort it 'cause I didn't know what it might do to me.

"Chop it up," said a friend, "mix it with pot and put it at the end of a cigarette."

I did it. I smoked it. I liked it.

"Cool," I said. "I can handle this."

It was fun.

Mind you, smoking cocaine over the years was never an everyday thing. Maybe once every six months. Never even bought the stuff. If someone offered, maybe I'd accept or maybe I wouldn't.

So there I was—a semi-regular smoker and once-in-a-while coker. Thought I had a lid on things. And I did. Until the beginning of the end of my marriage.

See, I'm a stone romantic. I love love; I love dreaming about love, thinking about love, writing about love, singing about love. I love being in love. I fell in love early, at age fourteen, with my childhood sweetheart, Claudette. I married her when I was nineteen. She was a member of the Miracles, and, for over three decades, the love of my life. Ours was a fairy-tale romance we thought would last a lifetime. But that lifetime proved limited. My heart was changing, my soul rearranging.

This all happened after coke had contributed mightily to

the demise of my friend and brother Marvin Gaye. You'd think I'd heed the warning. I didn't.

Instead, I started toying with rock cocaine.

"How's it work?" I asked the first time I saw it in late 1984.

Cat broke off a little chip, chopped it, mixed it with weed and put it in the end of a cigarette, just the way I liked it. Man, it smoked so smooth and got me so high, I called it the best shit I'd ever had.

Started buying little rocks, always mixed with weed and smoked in cigarettes. The cats call 'em primos. Never did use the pipe. Never needed to. Got hooked just the same.

In May of 1985, I left home. Leaving Claudette and the kids covered me with confusion and pain. It was a hurtful time, living alone in an apartment.

Folks who know me will tell you, I've never been a recluse. I'm outgoing, a people person, never one to sulk or stay to myself for long. But coke was changing me. Coke was filling in the empty spaces of my life. Slowly—then quickly —coke was taking over.

At first I'd start off with a gram rock, a bag of weed and a pack of cigarettes. That might last me three, four days. Then I'd lay off for three, four days, and still have some weed and cigarettes left over.

But then I'd get a gram and a half, and I'd be smoking more; I'd be staying in more; I'd be calling my man for more rocks, bigger rocks. If he came by at six at night, I'd run down for a pack of cigarettes to make twenty little coke concoctions. By midnight, though, I was back at the 7-Eleven buying another twenty cigarettes, and I'd be up all night, getting high, staying high, sleeping all day, letting the phone ring off the wall and paying no mind to nothing 'cept getting high again, looking to replace bad feelings with good feelings, only I was feeling worse and worse, till suddenly I weighed less than 130 pounds, which on a man over six feet tall can look awfully frightening.

I *was* frightened, I was sliding down to rock bottom, and there was nothing I could do. I was so skinny I'd have to pin my pants, hiding the pin under my shirttails, before I'd go out. And I was going out less and less.

My niece and assistant, Sharon, would call and cry over the phone.

"I hear it in your voice," she'd say. "You've been up all night. You've been smoking that cocaine."

"I have not!" I lied. "Get off my case, girl! Leave my ass alone!"

Normally patient, usually well-mannered, I was losing it, going off on the people I loved most.

ABC was doing a show on songwriters and asked to interview me. I agreed. I stayed sober during the interview, but later, watching myself on TV, I cried like a baby. My appearance was shocking: my jaws were sunken; my eyes protruded out of my head from loss of weight. Put some crossbones behind my head and I'd be the perfect pirate flag. Look at me and you'd see death warmed over.

Sitting there, I saw what was happening: I was killing myself. But the thought only made me reach for another primo.

Afraid to tell anyone about the cold sweats, the heart palpitations, the pus passing out of my body, I promised myself to stop.

But I only smoked more.

I heard warnings from on high. I vowed to heed those warnings.

But I didn't. I couldn't. I was trapped in hell and couldn't find a way out. I lacked the strength. Rock cocaine had destroyed my will and poisoned my mind. Rock cocaine was about to decimate my body and end my life—once a success—in shame.

How had this happened?

I'd always thought of my life as a series of awesome blessings. Yet my life had turned into an awesome failure.

How, in eighteen short months, had I gone from being a well-respected star to some funky junkie?

What had my life been about?

How had it all led up to this?

PART ONE

The Beginning

Roots

I can see Daddy standing there. I can hear his soothing baritone voice. It's a soft summer's day with the sun blazing down and the clouds floating by. We're fishing—our poles dangling in the water, our feet dangling off the pier—and Daddy's telling stories. He's a tall beautifully built honey-tanned black man with a deep, easy, country drawl. He always calls me boy.

"Boy," he says, "back in Selma, Alabama, things was different for black folk. Especially my family. See, my poppa—your grandfather—he was a powerful handsome man, but he was used. Owners turned him into a stud. Many a time they'd order him to mate with their prettiest lady slaves. Wanted 'em to turn out perfect kids who'd sell for big money. They kept using Poppa till he met a woman he loved. That turned out to be my mama. He stayed with her. Then history took over."

"What do you mean, Daddy?"

"Emancipation tripped up the slaveowner. He couldn't swoop up any of Poppa and Mama's kids. Twelve children were born, all free, and you're looking at one of them."

I was fascinated by my father's past. I loved asking him questions, yet the answers never quite satisfied.

"But why don't I know any of your family?" I'd inquire.

"Look, boy, I haven't seen hide nor hair of any of them since I was twelve. I already done told you that story."

"Tell it again."

"Well, I was working a paper route, and there was this bully, this big ol' white boy who'd beat up on me and steal my money. Now I wasn't the type to go crying to my older brothers. No, sir. I was gonna take care of this bad-ass myself. So I got me a penknife and waited till the next time he looked to mess with me. Sure enough, that time came quick. And when he started to take a swing at me, I cut him. Cut him deeper than I wanted. Cut his leg. He started bleeding and I started panicking 'cause back then no colored could draw blood from a white and live to tell 'bout it."

"Is that when you ran away?"

"Ran like the devil. Never turned around, not even to say good-bye to my folks. Just headed for the train tracks and prayed no harm would come to my family for what I did. But I wasn't thinking, I was just running for the first freight that came along. Jumped on and never looked back."

"Never saw any of your family again?"

"Not once."

"Doesn't that make you sad?"

"Boy, I thought we were supposed to be fishing, not thinking."

That was Daddy. Loved to fish so much, my niece called him "Daddy Fish." But his main nickname, given by his bowling-alley buddies, was Five.

Five was a sweetheart. He was generous. But he was also a Dr. Jekyll and Mr. Hyde. Booze did that. Split his personality in half until there were two daddies—the kind daddy and the crazy daddy, the peaceful daddy and the fighting daddy.

For instance, he'd take me out and get to drinking. We'd go to a joint called the Jackson Bar. He'd sit me up on the stool and start throwing back V.O. like it was water. Get all loud and rowdy and ready to destroy Detroit. Funny, he liked to fight his friends.

"Daddy," I'd say. "We better go."

And that'd be it. He'd chill, just 'cause I told him to.

Me and my niece Sylvia, whom he loved like a daughter, were the only people on God's earth who could keep Five from his bad self.

"Good thing my son's here," he'd tell some guy he was ready to wreck, "or I'd whup your sorry ass."

Daddy was plain folk. He read little more than the newspapers; he could be lewd and crude. Psychologically, I believe, he was wounded by his separation from his family. He talked tough. Fact is, he was tough.

"After I jumped that freight," he said, "I found me a little dog. Now me and that mutt made our way up north, hoboing around, working open markets. See, the dog was a ratter. He'd catch rats running through the fruits and vegetables. That's how we'd make a little money and move on. Did that for years until the dog died and I decided to settle down in a big city. By then it was 1919 and I was living in Cleveland, Ohio. That's the reason you see me rooting for the Cleveland Indians, the Cleveland Browns and every other goddamn Cleveland ball team. Even when I finally moved to Detroit and married your mother, Cleveland never left my heart."

As a kid I remember Daddy driving us to Cleveland to watch baseball games. The Indians had black players like Satchel Paige, and my soul filled with joy just to be with Five, eating popcorn and hot dogs and watching Larry Doby smack that little white ball beyond the big banks of blazing lights, sending it sailing all the way to the moon.

In the car home, resting my head on Daddy's shoulder, he'd tell me more stories, his voice deep and dark as night.

"In the thirties," he'd say, "bowling alleys got to be popular. That's when I got me a job as a pinsetter over at the Whittier Recreation Center. Now the alley was closed during the summer, so I helped out this car mechanic. Anything to stay alive. But come winter, I'd be back in the alley. That's where they started calling me 'Five' 'cause alley number five was my favorite. Wouldn't work any other. But I also wanted to get ahead. Boy, you always need to get ahead. I saw that the pin captain had charge over sleeping accommodations —back then bowling alleys had cots and showers—plus he sold sandwiches, cigarettes and wine. He oversaw all the alleys. He even had assistants. Hell, the pin captain made so much money in winter he could vacation all summer. Man, that's what I wanted to be—a pin captain!—and that's what I became. In no time I was making $70 a day and $200 on weekends. Got me enough money to buy a brand-new 1939 Buick right off the assembly line. And that was the car that caught your mama's eye."

Mama had a sharp eye and keen mind. She was a big-boned woman with light skin and a love of music, poetry and book-learning. She schooled herself. Her name was Flossie, and she was a powerful presence in the world.

Her father, Reverend Benjamin Smith, left her mother in Memphis, going up north to start a church. Grandpa's mother was a Caucasian French lady with interchangeable blue-green eyes, the source, according to Mama, of my eyes.

Mama dropped out of school in the eighth grade, but fashioned her own education. She was disciplined. Every day she'd learn to spell, pronounce and use a minimum of five new words. She loved language. In fact, she was fluent in two languages: English and Cuss.

She was wise and high-minded, but she was also down, a savvy street woman who could tongue-lash you into ribbons.

I remember, for instance, an older girl complaining to her about me. I was still in my walker when this child claimed I'd called her a "fucker-wucker."

Mama scolded me, but she couldn't go too far. That word, she knew, was her own invention.

Mama's life was her own invention. She wasn't one to be led around; she wasn't afraid; she was a tough-minded, bold and resourceful woman. Her lot hadn't been easy, but she offered no excuses and made no apologies.

She had two husbands and two daughters before marrying Daddy.

Her first beau, Alfred "Headneck" Bynum, wed her when she was only fifteen. Their union ended violently.

It happened one night when their baby girl, Geraldine, was only six months old. Mama was in the back holding Gerry in her arms when she heard a knock at the front door. Headneck went to answer.

Boom!

Mama's heart froze; she hurried towards the door, where she saw her husband thrown against the wall, his body sliding down, his eyes wide in horror, blood spurting from a gaping red hole in his stomach.

He'd been shot to death by a fellow worker named Nailface. They were both plasterers. Apparently Nailface was plastered on booze and, arguing over a crap game, went berserk. Face and Neck had been best friends.

At age eighteen, Mama took Gerry and moved to St. Louis, where she married a man she knew from Memphis, William Henry "Beamie" Ligon. Now Beamie was crazy jealous. And one night after a dance they fought until Mama fell down a flight of stairs. Whether he pushed her or she tripped, Mama never made clear. Either way, she was hurt. Beamie rushed her to the hospital where the doctor said there was no serious damage either to her or the baby.

The baby turned out to be my second sister, Rose Ella.

"I've had it with jealous men," said Mama. "I'm going home."

Back in Memphis, she lived with Grandma for a spell. In fact, Mama did Grandma a world of good. Not only taught her to read and write, but convinced her to apply for the money the U.S. Government owed her. Grandma's second husband died fighting in World War I, and she had benefits coming.

They finally came—but only after years of Mama doggedly pursuing the matter. Grandma used the money to remodel and Mama bought herself a grand piano. See, Mama had God-given talent—perfect pitch, a lovely contralto voice—and the neighbors would come 'round to hear her.

Mama was energetic; she was restless; she was fearless. And like so many other blacks back then, she thought her kids would have a better chance up north. She went to visit her cousins in Detroit and decided to stay. That's where she met my daddy, and that's how my life began.

Five was a player—he liked his women—but when he met Mama, he'd met his match.

Sure, he was a distinguished-looking cat, graying at the

temples. You might think he was a doctor or lawyer. But Mama was no slouch. In those days the criteria for a fox were fair skin, curly hair and big legs. Mama had it all, and Daddy was dazzled.

Here's how they hooked up:

Pop had a pal named Claude, a car mechanic, who looked so much like Five, you'd confuse 'em for brothers. Even had the same last name: Robinson. Now Claude knew about these fine-looking sisters—Babe, Bea and Catherine. They were Mama's cousins and, like Mama, they were superfine. They were having a party.

"I'm bringing you on this set," said Claude, " 'cause I know how you like the ladies."

"I'm ready," Five replied.

Soon as they arrived, Daddy took center stage, flirting flamboyantly, setting up the house by buying everyone drinks, throwing around money like there was no tomorrow.

At the same time he played it cool, lavishing attention on all the foxes except Flossie, the chick he wanted most.

"A bunch of fine talent," she told her cousins, using the street term for good looks, "wasted on a foolhardy man."

But the foolhardy man was a determined man. He did his homework, found out where Mama lived and even learned she had two daughters, the oldest of whom, Gerry, was pregnant with her first child. Most cats would have run. Not Daddy; Daddy hung.

When he showed up at Mama's, he was riding in style. His brand-new Buick was something to see.

Flossie, though, was no floozie. She was a tough judge of character and didn't trust the man. Said he wasn't her type. Said Five was jive.

But Five was also full of surprises. He'd charm the stripes

off a tiger. He'd show up at Mama's holding a big bouquet of sweet-smelling flowers and flanked by two of his pinboys carrying cartons of groceries. He even brought toys for Gerry's unborn baby. This was during the Depression, mind you, when money was minimal.

Mama, though, was tough. She refused the offerings.

"You got to accept," argued Five. "After all, I get the stuff wholesale."

Flossie was proud but practical. "You can buy my groceries for me wholesale, but only if you let me pay."

Once he had a hold, Daddy hung even tougher, coming by on Sundays, giving my sisters gifts and rides in his Buick. He ingratiated himself into the family. In early 1939, for instance, when Gerry's daughter Sylvia was born, Five passed out cigars and bragged until folks thought she was his own grandchild.

He won Mama's heart and Mama's hand. A year later, on February 19, 1940, I was born.

They were happy.

Three years later, they were divorced.

Colorful Confusions

I almost didn't make it.

Doctors urged Mama to abort, saying she was 33, hadn't given birth in a dozen years and suffered from high blood pressure.

But Mama wasn't intimidated by doctors. She wanted more information. So she went to the library, and when she couldn't find documented proof linking high blood pressure to birth defects, she went ahead.

Thank you, Mama.

Funny thing is that Mama arrived at the maternity ward just about the time her daughter Geraldine was leaving. A week earlier Gerry had given birth to her first son, Tyrone. Because Gerry was only sixteen and already had a daughter, Sylvia, Mama found a home for Tyrone in the family. He went to live with Uncle Dewey and Aunt Margarite, who were childless, in Chicago. Gerry's next child—another boy, born on the heels of Tyrone—was also adopted, this time by foster parents. Gerry's husband, Bill, was sick; they were being supported, in part, by the state and had no choice. Later, though, Bill and Gerry would have another seven kids, who they kept and raised.

My own birth made minor social history.

See, back then they were still segregating infants in northern hospitals, and spotting my pale blond fuzz, blue eyes and fair complexion, they classified me as white.

Can you imagine the stupidity of segregating little babies?

Meanwhile, Daddy was going nuts cause he couldn't find me in the black nursery.

And the nurses—black and white—were giggling behind Mama's back, figuring that this black woman had just given birth to a white baby.

But then Five arrived, and seeing how William Robinson Senior and Junior had the same face, down to the bags under their eyes, those wise-ass nurses had to shut up.

Ever since I can remember, Flossie and Five were fighting. Now you'd think that'd disturb me deeply, but I don't believe it did. Even though Daddy moved out when I was three, my parents handled it with such wisdom, carefully covering me with such love, that I survived their divorce with few scars.

"You didn't break our marriage," Daddy would remind me, "so don't try and fix it."

He made sure I didn't take the blame.

"The problem between her and me and the foolish things we did," I wrote thirty years later, inserting this theme in a song, "haven't got a thing to do with the love between me and my kids."

"Your father drinks, your father's crazy, but he loves you mightily," Mama would say.

"Flossie's always on my case," claimed Five. "I can't get along with that woman no way, but that doesn't mean she's not a fine mother. Boy, she loves you like nothing else in this world."

Even after their divorce, they supported each other when it came to me.

Mama would take me to the corner at the end of the block where I'd wait for Daddy to pick me up. He couldn't come on our street 'cause Mama took out a peace bond against him. She did that, I believe, not out of fear, but to punish him. Yet for all her anger, she never tried to keep him out of my life. And he remained there, as did she, for as long as they lived.

Why didn't they get along?

"He's too extravagant," Mama might say.

"She's too bossy," Daddy would declare.

In truth, Flossie could be overbearing. She was also too intellectual for Five. Daddy wasn't dumb—far from it—but his learning was limited, while Mama never stopped seeking knowledge.

Their marriage was a mismatch, and even though I was in the middle, I was always at the receiving end of their devotion; I never lacked for love.

Colorful language was an early stimulation for me. I was verbal from the get-go.

By age one I was talking. Walking came later, but I made do.

When I was still in a walker, Mama would send me to Mr. Henry's corner store to buy her cigarettes. If there was any change, she let me use it for ice cream.

First time there wasn't any change, I was slick enough to convince Mr. Henry to run a tab. Little by little, my little bill got bigger.

"What is this?" Mama wanted to know when Mr. Henry finally told her what she owed.

"Junior said it was all right."

"*Junior!* Henry, don't tell me you're taking orders from a baby boy?"

"That baby boy's pretty convincing, Flossie. You try to resist him."

Mama tried and Mama succeeded. Mama was plenty strict. But also plenty wise. With the right messages, Mama was always on time—and spoke in rhyme.

If I only half-cleaned my room, I'd hear, "Once a task is begun, don't leave until that task is done.

"Whether your job's big or small, do it well or not at all.

"From the time you're born till you ride the hearse, nothing's so bad that couldn't be worse," she said, comforting me in her arms after I'd been hit on the head with a horseshoe and thought the throbbing pain would never stop.

Once I was screaming for a toy I couldn't have. Man, I was carrying on something fierce before Mama ran down the story about the shoeless dude who felt bad till he met the man who had no feet. That one stuck with me for life.

Mama taught in proverbs, parables and poetry; her language was lighthearted and fun; she painted pictures with words.

Both my parents were storytellers, tireless talkers, and it's no wonder I turned out a writer.

For the first ten years of my life I was a happy kid, wildly in love with anything to do with cowboys and music. Strange combination? Maybe so, but that was me.

I loved the cowboys and I even loved their sidekicks—Hopalong Cassidy and Lucky, Roy Rogers and Gabby Hayes, the Lone Ranger and Tonto, the Cisco Kid and Pancho. These were my heroes. I had my hats, my toy guns, my cowboy boots, and soon, thanks to my Uncle Claude, I had me my name—*Smokey Joe!*

Claude was Pop's pal and a second father to me. He'd married Beulah, a gorgeous half-white woman, who was closer to me than any aunt. They were my godparents. In fact, I lived with them awhile, just after I was born, when Flossie and Five were both in the hospital having appendectomies at the same time.

Once when I was six or seven, Uncle Claude took me to a matinee—a cowboy movie of course—and asked afterwards, "How'd you like the picture, Smokey Joe?"

"Smokey Joe?" I asked.

"Yeah, ain't you Smokey Joe?"

"Yup, that's me!"

Man, I liked that a whole lot more than being called William or Junior.

Later I learned Uncle Claude was being ironic.

Dark-skinned blacks were sometimes called Smokey. I still had blond hair and blue eyes and was anything *but* smokey.

"I'm doing this," he was saying, "so you won't ever forget that you're black."

Back in my little-boy mind, though, color wasn't the issue—cowboys were. Believe me, I was a bad hombre. I had me a cowboy talk—"Howdy Pardners!"—and a cowboy walk—my knees slightly bent, heels turned over, thumbs hooked inside my genuine Red Ryder belt.

"Just call me Smokey Joe."

"I'm calling you crazy," said sister Rose Ella, who liked to taunt me.

"And I'm calling you Roserellis," I teased her back.

"And I'm calling you Junior like I always do," said Mama, who stuck to her word.

Home

We lived in a house on Belmont Street, one of those two-story jobs, that was plenty big. This was on the North End of Detroit, an old Jewish neighborhood turning black. When Flossie and Five bought our home, the area was nice, several cuts above the raw ghetto.

When Flossie and Five divorced, Mama kept the property. Gerry had a family of her own, and when Rose Ella was eighteen—and I was four—she also left. That meant Mama and I were alone. The upstairs flat was rented out to the Cook family; in our part, three bedrooms were occupied by boarders, the fourth shared by me and Mama.

I felt like an only child. Got loads of attention. Flossie had some boyfriends, chiefly a tall thin dude called Bones, but Bones didn't bother me. I was Mama's main man, and she lavished love on me like no one else. She also whipped my ass nearly every day.

Wasn't her fault. I needed it. Couldn't stay out of mischief.

"Don't be climbing over that picket fence, Junior," she'd warn.

And sure enough, the next minute I'd be jumping the fence, paying her no nevermind.

One day, I remember, I was jumping when my pants leg caught on a picket. I wound up hanging upside down, crying for Mama to free me.

Here she comes, running out of the house, scared to death, thinking I've been bit by a snake or struck by lightning.

"What in heavens is wrong, Junior?"

She sees my predicament, though, and, just like that, her tone changes. She calms down and studies the situation while I'm still twisting and screaming for help.

"So," she says ever so slowly, "you tried to jump the fence."

"Just get me down," I'm crying, "please let me down, Mama."

"Didn't I tell you not to jump that fence?"

"Yeah, Mama, you told me, and I'm sorry, but I gotta get down, just get me down."

"I'm not sure what I'm going to do about this," she says, deliberating like a judge.

I'm still pleading and crying—"Get me down! Let me down!"—when Mama finally renders her verdict. "I'll tell you what I'm going to do. I'm going to walk to the side of the house and find me a switch, a great big switch. Don't move now, Junior, 'cause I'm coming back, and when I do, I'm gonna whip your ass good."

And, believe me, she did.

Daddy whipped me only once. After I'd seen a Tarzan movie I was so excited that me and a buddy started wrestling with butcher knives. I fell and sliced my elbow on a rock. Daddy spanked me good—not for wrestling, but for playing with knives—and then rushed me to the hospital for stitches.

Both my parents were powerful protectors.

Mama was especially watchful over me, yet ever since my birth she was never completely well. High blood pressure plagued her. She was a heavy woman—maybe 200 pounds —and also smoked. In those days few folk knew the damage cigarettes were doing. She was often tired, needed lots of rest and sometimes got so sick I'd be scared.

Despite everything, though, Mama drudged on. For a while she was a maid at the Leland Hotel. I'd tag along and help, sticking mountains of sheets and pillowcases in the big laundry basket.

Mama also sold corn whiskey to neighbors, right out of our house.

Our home was always filled with what we called nigger kin, friends close enough to be family.

There was also another cast of characters, an endless parade of people passing through our house, folks Mama might be trying to help—junkies, whores, drunks.

The junkies would be scratching themselves and nodding out, the whores would be strutting, but the drunks were the most pitiful—peeing on themselves, talking to folks who weren't there and looking to fight. It was wild.

Down at Poppa's place the pinboys gave me another view of things—raw and funny. Cats like Shorty and Hamp, who looked like an old prizefighter with a smashed-in nose and cuts all up his cheeks, were part of my life until they died.

At the same time, my upbringing was righteous. Mama was a churchgoer, a choir member. She'd be there Sunday and during the week as well. Naturally, she dragged me along. Although as a child I felt close to God—God gave me a warm glow, a feeling of faith—I didn't dig church. In Mama's Baptist sanctuary the sisters were fired up, shouting and shivering with such spirit that I grew frightened.

Religion ran all over our neighborhood, coming at me in strange and unexpected ways. For instance:

Picture Detroit in the winter of 1946: Snow's falling from a pale pearl-gray sky. A bitter wind's blowing, and everywhere you look Packards and Studebakers are slowly crunching down the slushy streets.

That's six-year-old me, oblivious to the weather, skipping along, going to play with my pal Richard Ross, who lives on Boston Boulevard, just a block over from Belmont.

"Hey, Rich."

"Hi, Smoke."

"Who's this guy?"

"Cecil."

"Where you from, Cecil?"

"Just moved from Buffalo."

"Let's go play in the rabbit field," Rich suggests.

The three of us hop over to Oakland Avenue, where we run 'round a vacant lot overgrown with weeds.

"Wanna see my new house?" asks Cecil.

"Why not?"

"That's it."

He points to a beautiful mansion next to the field.

"Come on in."

I approach the huge house hesitantly. Once inside, I'm awestruck—oil paintings, velvet tapestries, silk curtains, mahogany cabinets filled with ornate objects of silver and gold. Man, I've never seen nothing like this before!

We tiptoe down a long hallway, following the haunting strains of beautiful piano music.

Who's playing?

We poke our heads into the music room, and I'm amazed. Seated behind the baby grand is a baby herself, singing like an angel.

"That's my sister Aretha," says Cecil Franklin.

"What does your father do?" I ask.

"Preach."

"His daddy's Reverend C. L. Franklin," Rich remarks. "He's famous."

Aretha's only three. And with her are her sisters—eight-year-old Erma and baby Carolyn.

That's how I met the Franklin family.

Cecil's been my buddy all my life. So has Aretha. I fell in love with her when she was seven. But that's another story.

The story of my home life should be viewed like a musical. The sounds of music—dance music, jazz music, gospel music—wafted through our house, mingling with the sweet fragrances from Mama's kitchen.

The Victrola never stopped cooking. We had Sarah Vaughan for breakfast and rib roast for dinner; Nat Cole for lunch and fried chicken for supper. Billie Holiday and Billy Eckstine might be stewing all day long. The music Mama loved best —big bands, blues belters—was always simmering.

Mama also loved spirituals. I knew the sightless soul of the Five Blind Boys, the tight harmonies of the Mighty Clouds of Joy, the virtuosity of the Violinaires. Over at Reverend

Franklin's, playing with Cecil or flirting with Aretha, I might actually hear Clara Ward herself singing in their kitchen.

My own debut performance took place between Detroit and Memphis at age three:

World War II was happening and the train was jammed with soldiers. Me and Mom were on our way to visit Grandma. I was an outgoing little guy, strolling up and down the aisles, singing to myself. The army cats thought I was cute. They'd give me oranges and apples, picking me up on their laps, saying, "This is my man."

"Sing, little buddy," someone requested.

That's all I needed to hear.

"Jelly, jelly, jelly," I sang in my squeaky-voiced approximation of Billy Eckstine. "Jelly stays on my mind, drove my Mama crazy, drove my daddy stone blind."

Cats cracked up.

Mama was embarrassed. "What you doing, Junior, singing that song?"

"We like the way he sings," said the soldiers.

But by then, Mama was hurrying me back to my seat.

"Hurry, Mama," I begged her when I saw these kids on stage trying to sing. "I wanna go up there."

We were at the Michigan State Fair, and I wasn't any older than six.

"What you need to go up there for, Junior?"

"'Cause I wanna sing!"

"Well, if you wanna sing that bad . . ."

"I do."

And I did. Sang "Ragtime Cowboy Joe" until the folks cheered so loud I got scared. But I loved it, and so did Mama.

Afterwards we learned a man had made a record of it. And don't you know that Mama took that record home and proudly played it over the phone for everyone she knew.

Since that time she encouraged me, seeing how I'd wake up singing every morning, making up melodies at night, scribbling down little lyrics. I loved lyrics. I loved looking to see who wrote songs.

I also loved *Your Hit Parade* TV show. Couldn't wait till it came on. I liked the singers—Snooky Lanson, Giselle MacKenzie and Dorothy Collins. I'd sit in front of the tube with my *Hit Parade* magazine, following all the words. Fascinated me to watch the way they turned the tunes into little plays. I also loved seeing the songs fighting each other for the number-one spot.

Early on, starting with cowboy tunes, my musical taste was wide. One of my favorite songs in life, for example, was Kay Starr spinning that "Wheel of Fortune." When Daddy and I went fishing in Canada, I'd play it on the jukebox so many times, they'd throw us out of the restaurant.

Mama had an old upright at home, and I'd be banging it, figuring out simple melodies and chord combinations. Didn't know what I was doing—even though I was doing then what I do now, looking for ways to express myself.

As a kid, though, my favorite expressions were still those spoken by the cowboys, my mumble-mouthed heroes. My western obsession grew until I was telling everyone that when I grew up I was going to be a cowboy. Mama, who planned for me to be an educated professional, started worrying.

Then she got an idea.

Cowpokes and
Puppy Love

"Take him out west, Five," I heard Flossie say. "Let him see what it's really like."

"You really think it'd do him good?"

"Couldn't hurt none. And once he sees that there's no Roy Rogers out there chasing Indians, maybe the boy'll come to his senses. Get more serious about things."

"If you say so."

"I know so."

Was I hearing right? Was it possible? Were Mama and Daddy, long divorced, actually agreeing about something? Was I really about to see the Great American West?

We left on a scorching day in June of 1947, just the two of us, with me feeling like the luckiest kid alive. That winter the action at the bowling alley had been so good that Daddy could take off two months, devoted to me and our western trip.

Here we go, y'all!

Cruising in Five's new, blue, heavy-horsepowered black-fendered Caddie, Route 66 looked mighty slick.

First stop, St. Lou, a little strange 'cause there weren't hotels for blacks. But leave it to Five; he knew a lady with a boardinghouse, and, as usual, we were cool.

Gotta give Five a lot of skin for this trip. Poor cat drove and drove and drove, all on skinny two-lane highways. I'd be in the back seat playing, but mostly I'd be sleeping.

From St. Lou we hit Dallas, El Paso and Tucson.

"Got a girlfriend in Tucson," Five informed me. "You'll like her."

Miss Esther was her name and—like most of Daddy's ladies—she was a beauty. Had respiratory problems, though, which was why she lived in a dry climate. It was a strange scene. She stayed on a spread in the desert with a black family named the Whites who had a family of Chicanos working their land.

While I was there, Dennis and Leo, two of the Chicano boys my age, took me to a public swimming pool. They got in, but I didn't; I was turned away 'cause of my color. Standing outside the gate under the blazing sun, dying of heat while my pals were swimming, splashing and having a ball, I did a slow burn, remembering the summer before in Memphis:

Mama and I had gone to visit Grandma. Me and some buddies were coming back from a candy store when a group of white guys got all up in our faces.

"Niggers!" they started yelling.

"You think you white," one of 'em taunted me, " 'cause you got blue eyes."

I ignored this ignorant shit. *Sticks and stones*, I was thinking to myself. Just then, though, the kid made a mistake. He spit in my face. Being from Detroit, I couldn't let this go by; couldn't help myself; I kicked his ass. Whupped him bad.

My friends had to pull me off, and when we got back to Grandma's and Mama learned what happened, she started packing.

"You go beating on white folk," she said, "and you find yourself in a mess of trouble."

That same afternoon we headed back for Detroit. In a funny way I felt like Five running out of Selma after cutting up that white bully.

By the time me and Daddy got to Los Angeles, though, the taste of prejudice was gone. To me California looked like heaven. Never seen such green grass, blue skies, tall trees and gorgeous girls. They even had a Western shop. Daddy bought cowgirl boots to take back to Sylvia and I got me a mess of shirts and jeans.

Went as far down as Tijuana, then turned around and took the same route home, father and son exploring America together. It was a great life experience, a warm way of growing closer to Daddy. But I also missed Mama something fierce, and couldn't wait to get home and tell her every last detail of my two-month adventure.

Did it cure me of my cowboy mania? I'm not sure, but something else was starting to occupy my mind, another obsession, which, unlike the western thing, would never go away: women.

Girls, females, foxes—I've been fascinated with the opposite sex since I saw they existed. I was no older than three when I had my first sweetheart, Patty Harris. Used to take my nickels and walk her to the store, holding her hand, where I'd buy her ice-cream cones.

Mama would tease me. "That your girlfriend, Junior?"

"Sure is," I'd say, not in the least embarrassed. "I'm going to marry her."

My first day of school is a prime example of the powerful effect of females on my soul:

Mama takes me to kindergarten, but I won't stay.

"Don't leave me!" I'm crying, pulling at her dress.

"I'll be back for you at two o'clock," she assures me.

"No!" I carry on, sobbing like a baby. "I wanna go with you."

"You're staying, Junior, and that's it!"

She's gone and I'm still weeping when the teacher says, "Marva Jean, William is new to the class. Why don't you show him how we carry our chairs?"

Suddenly, like a vision out of a dream, this angelic-looking little girl with long black hair floats across the room and gently picks up a chair from behind. Everything about her appears exotic—her skin, her mouth, her dewy eyes. My tears stop falling and my love starts flowing. Forget Mama. I'm a goner for Marva Jean and can't wait to go to school every day, just to see her, as I'd sing much later in my life, just to touch her, I would do anything.

In second grade Marva Jean gave way to Marilyn Tinsley, another knockout but with beautifully braided brown hair. She wore neat little dresses and had heavenly hazel eyes. I loved Marilyn so much that I bought her a ring for a nickel from a dispenser at Mr. Henry's store. Even had a pink stone. Put it on her desk at school and watched her slip it on her finger, flashing a smile that lit me up like a light bulb. Only problem was that two days later her little finger turned a gruesome green.

I loved Aretha Franklin. Not only was she a cutie pie, but her musical talent was phenomenal. Me and my friends fooled with music, but none of us, like little Aretha, could sit down and play two-fisted full-blooded stomp-down piano. As a child, she played nearly as good as she plays now— that's how advanced she was. In fact, my feelings for Aretha were so strong that Cecil could hustle me for favors just by saying, "I'll fix you up with Ree." Finally, getting hip to his hype, I saw he had no intention of fixing me up; he was too much of a protective big brother. I was heartbroken.

Such were the rituals of romance.

I was a starry-eyed kid touched by feminine wiles—their smooth skin, their tender touch.

Mama couldn't complain 'cause I was also doing great in school. Made the honor roll every time. This gave Mama special joy. Because Gerry dropped out of high school, there was pressure on Rose Ella to do well. And she did. She was a brilliant student, getting straight A's at Cass Technical High, where entry requirements for blacks were superstiff. Rose Ella went on to Wayne State as a pharmacy major but, much to Mama's disappointment, quit to get married. As a scholastic hopeful, that left only me. And I wasn't about to disappoint my mother.

Little did I expect, though, that something deeper than disappointment awaited me, something so devastating, so completely crushing, I wasn't sure I'd ever recover.

When I was ten my world fell apart. Mama died.

Dazed

Those headaches, she said, were killing her.

I heard her, I saw her hurting, but I always thought the pain would pass. I didn't know that her blood pressure was so high the doctors couldn't measure it.

In 1950 her headaches got worse. My sisters took her from one hospital to another, yet she'd always come home. For long stretches of time she'd be bedridden, but eventually she'd bounce back.

Then, in October, she deteriorated. I should have seen it coming, but I turned the other way, denying what was happening, convincing myself that Mama would go on forever. There couldn't be a world without Mama.

"Mama wants to see you," Gerry told me on an evening when the whole family was huddled around, even Five, who stayed nearby during these last days.

I went up to her bedroom. She drew me close to her. I could see the awful pain in her eyes.

"Baby," she said, bringing me to her breast, "I just wanted to see you before you went to bed. I want you to know I love you. I'll always love you."

"I love you, too, Mama."

She kissed me gently—she had such little strength left —and sent me off to sleep.

I never saw my mother alive again.

She died that night, but it was decided not to tell me till morning. The next day, though, in all the confusion, I slipped out of the house and was off to school before anyone had a chance to let me know what had happened. I learned in a way that made it worse.

When I got to the homeroom, a strange hush fell over the class. The kids looked at me funny, like something was wrong. Word had spread through the neighborhood. They knew Mama was gone. Even the teacher knew.

"Let's have a moment of silent prayer for William," she said. "Though he lost his mother last night, he's come to school to be with his friends."

I jumped up, screaming, "I didn't lose my mama! My mama's home!"

"I'm so sorry, William," said the teacher.

"You're wrong!" I insisted. "I saw her last night!"

She came over and gave me a hug, whispering, "I think you better go home, Smokey." She'd never called me Smokey before.

Some friends accompanied me, and when I turned the corner off Oakland onto Belmont, I saw all these people carrying packages of food into the house.

I bolted, running up the steps and dashing into the living room. There were my sisters, my daddy.

"Mama's not dead, is she?" I asked.

"She died last night," someone said.

"No! She did not! I saw her! I kissed her! She's only sleeping! I can wake her up! Let me wake her!"

All morning long, I kept saying the same thing—"I'll wake her! Let me wake her!"—but slowly my screams turned to sobs when I saw the truth: There'd be no awakening. Mama was no more.

"She died of a cerebral hemorrhage," I heard someone say.

She was forty-three.

When I touched her in the casket, she was cold. Where once her flesh was cuddly and warm, she now felt like wax. Her skin was hard, and I drew back my hand, shocked by the horrible finality of it all.

"I know how you feel," said Gerry through her tears, "but I had her longer than you. I knew her better and I miss her more."

I didn't care what anyone said. I was numb from the pain, confused by the fear, dazed by the loss.

Daddy didn't help. Though she'd divorced him seven years ago, he mourned Mama as though they were still married. The days after her death he stayed drunk, drowning his grief, incapable of comforting me.

Nothing anyone did or said meant jack shit to me anyway.

All I knew was that my main person was gone, the woman who'd been with me night and day, making my meals, teaching me manners, punishing me, praising me, raising me as best she could.

I'd never felt this alone and frightened.

The fighting started the evening of the funeral, and then things only got worse.

We were all sitting around when the issue of the house came up. Turned out that Mom had left the house to me and my sisters, but Daddy wanted it for himself.

"It's ours," said Rose Ella, picking a bad time to pursue the matter. Five was a little juiced.

"It's my goddamn house," he said. "I paid for it."

"She got it when you divorced her," Rose Ella argued. "And she gave it to us."

Five flipped. His eyes got wide and his temples started throbbing; you could see the veins in his neck. Without warning, he picked up a butcher knife and went after Rose Ella, chasing her around the house, screaming, "This is my motherfucking house and I'm gonna live here and no one's gonna stop me!"

Fortunately, Rose Ella's husband, Chunky, caught Five, disarming the madman before he could do any harm.

I was caught in the middle—mourning, mixed up, my heart hurting. With Mama gone, I wanted Daddy around. Yet I hated the feuding and fighting.

The plan was for me to go live with Rose Ella and for Gerry's family to stay in Mama's house.

But Five beat 'em all to the punch. Day after the funeral, he slipped in, bringing along his girlfriend, Mary, to help with the cooking. Daddy wouldn't even let my sisters in the house.

My sisters fought back. They went to court where the judge not only awarded them the house, but also custody of me. Now Gerry—I called her Big Sister—was my legal guardian.

Daddy didn't contest the order, but, man, he got messed

up behind it. He was drinking and he was angry and when Big Sister finally came to move in—she and her family had been living in the projects—I started crying 'cause I didn't want my Daddy Five to leave.

"Why you turning him out?" I asked, turning on Gerry.

"I'm not. I want him to stay," she said. "The Cooks moved out from upstairs. He can stay up there if he wants to."

"Ain't gonna stay nowhere 'round here," Daddy declared. "Ain't gonna stay where I ain't wanted."

I started crying louder.

"For God's sake, Daddy," said Big Sister, "can't you see Junior wants you here?"

"Yeah, I could have told you that months ago."

"We had to do it legally. We had to take possession of the house. But we all want you to stay here."

"You got possession of the house, but you don't got possession of me."

"Stay," I begged.

"If I stay," he said, finally relinquishing, "it'll be only because of the boy, and, mind you, I'm only staying for a few months."

He stayed for twenty-three years.

Healing

Took awhile, but eventually I felt like I had another lease on life, another family, only this one bigger and louder and, in every way, more exciting than my first.

Maybe it was the shock of the change, the contrast in households, that helped me past my grieving.

Imagine: I'd gone from being Mama's only live-in child to having six noisy nosey siblings running 'round the house. I loved it. After all, this was family; I'd been close to these people since Jump Street. My nieces and nephews were my sisters and brothers. Sylvia and Sharon were among my favorite people on earth. I liked playing with Brenda, Billy, Jackie and baby Clifford. Big Sister stepped right in and became my mom. She was loving and understanding. At the time she came to Belmont, she was pregnant with Roger. Ten years later, Keith came along. Until I left home these were the folk who saved me from loneliness and made up for the loss of Mama.

Daddy stayed upstairs and, though it might seem strange, his roommate was Mama's second husband, Rose Ella's father, Beamie Ligon. The two dudes got along famously.

To make matters cozier, Tyrone, who'd been born just a week before me and was adopted by my aunt and uncle in Chicago, came back to live with us. He became my running buddy; we grew close as twins.

Not that there wasn't some strain: Five, for instance, went off on Big Sister from time to time, mostly, I believe, 'cause she looked like Mama.

And then the money got funny—so funny, in fact, that at Christmas the Good Fellows, a charity, would bring us a few clothes and toys.

See, my brother-in-law Bill, Gerry's husband, worked in a factory, where he'd suffered a back injury. He hurt so bad that we'd have to roll him out of bed and straighten him up each morning. But he had all these kids to support—me included—and somehow the cat did it. In spite of the back-breaking pain, he went to work.

Things also got rough for Daddy. Automatic pinspotters were on the rise. An era was dying. Five was no longer boss of the bowling alleys; his little empire was being taken over by machines.

He found other gigs, working as a car mechanic and driving a tar truck for the city. He always managed to slip me $5 a week for school money. I needed more—I had records and *Hit Parade* magazines to buy, I had girls to date—but I wasn't about to ask brother-in-law Bill for a dime. Bill had enough worries without me on his back.

So at age eleven I went to work, delivering packages in my little wagon for Mr. Hackerman's grocery store. Also helped a pal on a paper route deliver the Detroit *Free Press* at night. My first real job, though, came when I was twelve. Mrs. Wiggins had bought Mr. Henry's store, renaming it Two Sisters Unique. She hired me as an all-around helper, cleaning the counters, floors and windows three days a week.

*　　　*　　　*

I still loved school. And teachers like Mrs. Harris made me love it even more. She was this wonderful old white woman with silver-gray hair who started the Young Writers' Club. She encouraged us to create little stories, poems and sketches, and, man, she'd be displaying some of my work nearly every week in the hallway, even my drawings. I had me a Big Ten notebook where I'd also be jotting down songs. Mrs. Harris was one of the first to make me see the value of writing.

I was writing, and I was also singing. From the start those two activities were hooked up in my heart. Words rhymed easily in my imagination, and I tried to sing with good articulation.

My musical training started in fifth grade. Sang in the glee club. Hell, we'd be chirping *everywhere*—skipping down the hallways, jumping 'round the gym, joking in the bathrooms. Had me a quartet. Even wrote our eighth-grade graduation play, a musical, about the consequences of dropping out of school too soon.

Formed another group in junior high, this one with Cecil, Michael Fitzgerald and Floyd Birch. Saw the power of music when I wrote a campaign song for a girl named Naomi who was running for class president. Michael and Cecil, Detroit's slickest dancer, did the Chicken while our harmony brought down the house. Naomi won by a landslide.

That night at Cecil's house, we were celebrating the victory when in walked Reverend Franklin with Aretha. They'd just come off a gospel tour. Mind you, Aretha wasn't even a teenager yet.

"Hey, Ree, where y'all coming from?"

"Chicago, Memphis and St. Louis."

I could see she was a little tired, but she still joined in the merriment. Aretha's shy, but fun-loving, especially when she knows you well.

"Hey, guess what," she offered, "I met Fats Domino."

"Fats Domino! Wow! What was he doing on a gospel show?"

"He wasn't, but I meet all kinds of people, Smoke. There's a lot of stuff happening out there on the road. Sometimes it's even more than I want to see."

She turned her eyes from me and gazed out the window, looking like a wise woman in the body of a child.

Child's play was just about behind me by the time I got to high school. Music, like girls and sports, had become an obsession. Let me tell you why.

Under the Influence

My musical roots run back to a single source: Sarah Vaughan. Sarah was the foundation.

Long before I'd heard rock 'n' roll, Sarah was part of my household. I adored her. I idolized her. I found her sound —her perfect enunciation, her lavish phrasing—soothing and sensuous. Man, when Sarah sang, I swooned. I emulated her lush licks, her tasty turns, her jazz jumps, her incredible range. I loved the way she cried with her voice; I was awe-struck by her subtlety and sensitivity. No wonder they called her the Divine One. Sarah did shit that killed me.

So it was a woman who shaped my style.

But I wondered: *Should a cat like me be singing like a chick?* I soon had my answer.

The mid-fifties came along and so did the Age of Rock 'n' Roll. First group that slayed me was Billy Ward and the Dominoes. I thought their hit song "Have Mercy, Baby" was sung by a woman till I went down to see them at the Broadway Capitol Theater.

Man, was I surprised!

There, onstage, Clyde McPhatter was singing lead in a

voice high enough to be a chick. The chicks, though, not only dug it, they were going absolutely nuts—hysterical, crying, screaming, throwing themselves at Clyde's feet! I was loving it too 'cause Clyde was so soulful. Musically, he made a huge impression on my heart.

Around the same time I'd heard a Detroit group called Nolan Strong and the Diablos. Like Clyde, Nolan was a first tenor driving women wild. How much more motivation did I need?

Add Frankie Lymon and Sam Cooke to the stew, another pair of sweet-and-spicy high-voiced influences.

Early on I saw that my own singing voice, so naturally high, might have some guys calling me girlish, but who cared when the girls ate it up like candy?

I was raised in a dazzling din of doo-wop, seduced by the silver sounds of Harvey and the Moonglows—me and my pals would memorize their background blends—the Dells, Flamingos, Spaniels, Sonny Til and the Orioles, Lee Andrew and the Hearts. Heavenly harmony—five different parts merged like magic—was in the air. Pleasing the ear was the aim. The Four Aims, later the Four Tops, was the baddest group around. I was raised when the quality of street music was extremely high. There was no screaming, no faking, no farting around. If you couldn't sing, forget it; but if you could, women were yours.

I remember once looking out the window and seeing this long limo arriving on our block.

Who is it? I asked myself, thinking it had to be the mayor or governor. Turned out to be someone even more important—Jackie Wilson.

Jackie was a local hero, the cat who took Clyde McPhatter's place with the Dominoes. He'd been a leader of the Shakers, one of Detroit's most notorious gangs. He'd also been a Golden Glove boxer. He could sing high, low and every which way; with his smooth moves and natural polish, he could outdance Fred Astaire. He was rugged handsome, had processed hair and big flashy eyes. When I saw him that day on our street visiting his cousins, it was like seeing some god.

See, in my neighborhood, we idolized the entertainers, the preachers and the pimps. They were the ones with the sharp clothes, the Cadillac cars, the fine women. They had the glory.

It was glory we were seeking at Northern High School when we formed a group called the Five Chimes—glory, or at least the love of ladies.

This was the group that would eventually evolve into the Miracles. The first formation was me, Warren "Pete" Moore —I'd known Pete since we were thirteen—Clarence "Humble" Dawson, James "Rat" Grice and Donald Wicker.

Wick was soon replaced by Ronnie White. Ron lived across the street from Rat. I'd known him from way back; at age eleven he'd been our paperboy and powerfully interested in Sylvia.

When Humble quit we replaced him with Emerson "Sonny" Rogers. This group was good enough to win Ed McKensie's local TV talent contest. We wanted to stay fixed on five voices. But five became four again when Rat revealed wedding plans. His chick was pregnant and, as far as singing, Rat was history.

"Got a cousin," said Sonny, "who sings his ass off."

"Bring him 'round to rehearsal," I said.

Bobby Rogers rounded out the group. We were set—Bobby, Pete, Ron, Sonny and Smokey. We practiced hard. Even changed our name to the Matadors, thinking that sounded more manly.

Manliness was important to me. I wouldn't call myself arrogant, but certainly confident. I was good at most sports. I saw myself as an athlete. You should have seen me. Man, I was doing just great till I got the shit knocked out of me.

I survived, but barely.

The Boy with the
Golden Hubcaps

It was just a scrimmage, but I took it seriously. I'd played basketball, but I'd lettered in varsity football. Football was my game. Coach put me on defense 'cause of my attitude: *To get past me, you'll have to kill me.*

One cat did.

Name was John Oliver, a six-foot-three dude who weighed 200 pounds. At the time, I was five foot ten and weighed 150. We were practicing and he was running at me—all I had to do was push him out of bounds—when I started thinking, *Smokey, you gonna fuck this cat up, you gonna collide with him just to see what happens.*

POW!

When I came to, I was seeing stars.

"Give Robinson room to breathe," Coach was warning. "Nobody touch him."

He couldn't take me to the hospital without my legal guardian, Gerry, so the guys put me on a stretcher, slipped me in the back of a station wagon and drove me home. My side was aching like I'd been hit by a truck. Later I learned that I'd fractured my ribs.

When we arrived at Belmont, Beamie was on the porch. Beamie was Mama's second husband and something of a character. Liked wearing those little snap-on golf caps. Liked wisecracking.

"Damn, Junior," he said, "you look like you're sure-enough hurt."

Barely able to talk, I grunted.

"What happened?" Beamie wanted to know.

". . . threw a body block . . . messed up my side . . ."

"What position were you playing, boy?"

"Cornerback."

"Tell you what, Junior. Next year you tell the coach you want to play *way* back."

Way back in my childhood, I was struck by something more powerful than a flying fullback. I was hit by love, a lifetime love that struck me and stuck to me like honey. Here's how the honey started dripping and I started tripping:

When I was fourteen, a year before John Oliver ruined my ribs, the Five Chimes were going to Sonny Rogers's to rehearse. Hadn't been there before. I was curious about the street he lived on 'cause it was called Warren Court. I expected to see fabulous mansions, like on Boston Boulevard, where Cecil and Aretha stayed, but all I saw was an unpaved country-looking road on the outskirts of Black Bottom, Detroit's poorest section. There were but six houses on the whole block.

Sonny was there to greet us.

"Come on in. I want you to meet my sister and mom. They're down in the basement."

If I were to paint portraits from my life, this would be one of the big ones:

In the middle of the canvas you'd see two women, two gorgeous women, mother and daughter, Viola and Claudette, covered in white. They're wearing aprons, holding paintbrushes and, despite the fact that their faces are covered with whitewash, they seem a study in beauty.

They were busy whitewashing the basement that morning, but somehow the drudgery of the job made them appear even more radiant. They were both ravishing—Viola voluptuous, Claudette petite and pretty. Claudette had a gentle, exquisite aura, big brown eyes, a littlebitty waistline and nice rounded hips. It wasn't just her mouth that smiled, it was her whole face. She was a cutie pie, a fox, flipping me out the first time I saw her.

For a year I loved her from afar. I had other girlfriends, and even lost my virginity, but not with Claudette. Claudette was unapproachable. She was almost too beautiful, too angelic. She was also deeply shy and absolutely brilliant in school. I was smitten, but intimidated. She was around us all the time. She had a lovely singing voice and was a great dancer. In fact, together with Bobby's sister Jeanette and two other girls, Gwen and Margie, she started a sister group called the Matadorettes. But somehow I could never get next to her, until . . .

The summer of 1955. The gang was all there, celebrating Claudette's birthday over at the Rogers's house on Warren Court.

I couldn't keep my eyes off the birthday girl, the way her face lit up when she laughed, the way her eyes smiled, the way she walked and talked so softly, the way she danced so sweet and sexy. Finally I asked her to go out on the front porch.

There was a warm breeze in the air. The night was clear, the city quiet. We heard muffled noises from the party, the kids slow-dancing to Johnny Ace's "Pledging My Love."

"Happy birthday, Claudette."

"Thanks, Smokey."

"By the way, how old are you?"

"Eighteen."

Holy shit, I thought to myself. *She's three years older than me! I don't have a chance with this chick!*

Later I learned that she was pushing her age up. In truth, she'd just graduated from Commerce High School at fifteen. She was so smart, she'd skipped three years; she would've skipped four if Viola hadn't complained that they were accelerating her too quickly.

"Look, Claudette," I said, building up nerve. "I really like you."

"You do?" She sounded genuinely surprised.

"I do. I really really like you."

"I never knew."

"And I'd like to . . . well, I'd like to kiss you good-night. Would that be okay?"

She hesitated, considering my request. "You can kiss me good-night, Smokey."

I reached out to her—my heart pounding like crazy—our lips met, but when I tried to slip my tongue in her mouth, she clamped up and pulled back.

"What's wrong?" I asked.

"I don't want to kiss you like that."

"I'm sorry," I said, seeing her inexperience when it came to sex, "but can I take you out sometime?"

"I'd like that," she assured me.

*   *   *

Our first real date wasn't till four months later, in November. It was Thanksgiving and her mom had invited me to dinner. Later, Claudette remembered me trying to scoop up my peas with a knife. I was sure nervous, but also thrilled to be seated next to her, even with her folks and brother around. Anything to be close to Claudette.

We started dating—ice-skating at Palmer Park, bowling at the Twenty Grand, dancing at the Madison Ballroom. Soon I came down on her for sex. I didn't have a chance. Claudette was naive, but intent on saving herself for marriage. I didn't like that; I was ready and raring to go.

"I'll have to deal with some other girls," I explained.

"If that's what you have to do," she replied, "do it."

And I did. With a little help from Daddy.

When I was eleven, Five taught me to drive. Took me to this resort area in Canada and showed me on his standard-shift 1950 Ford.

When I was sixteen Five took me by surprise, arriving home in an old 1946 Ford.

"Whose car is that?" I wanted to know.

"Yours."

"*What!*"

"Go ahead and drive it."

Like a jet pilot leaping into the cockpit, I flew behind the wheel and zoomed 'round the neighborhood, honking at my friends to pile in. There was room for three up front, four could squeeze in the back and, even though Five warned against it, some pals rode the running boards.

"This is the Hawk," I told my partners, the name coming to me in a flash.

The Hawk was my baby. The Hawk represented a new

kind of freedom, a leap from being a boy to a playboy, a guy who could cruise anywhere he wanted. The Hawk was deep.

I treated the Hawk like a partner. The Hawk became my best friend. I talked to the Hawk. I even dressed the Hawk, working extra hard to buy accessories I considered especially cool.

I was earning money at Mrs. Wiggins's Two Sisters Unique. Also worked as a messenger for Western Union. And I was into hair processing. See, Cecil Franklin had been doing the doos for the boys in the neighborhood. He charged less than the barbershops—$2.00 against their $7.00—and his work was fantastic. He showed me how to make the waves with a comb and then set it with my finger. Soon I became a skilled doo-er myself. When Cecil went off to Morehouse College, he turned his clientele over to me.

With the extra bread I bought a sander and primed the Hawk gray, a hip move in those days. I also bought some stick-on phony whitewalls and painted my hubcaps gold. One girl started calling me the boy with the golden hubcaps. I liked that.

I liked anything that brought me to the attention of the girls. And though I was enjoying sex with a couple of chicks, my thoughts stayed on Claudette. She was my heart. She was also driving me crazy.

Claudette had her act together. She had a job as Executive Secretary to the director of the Detroit YMCA. She'd won awards for shorthand and typing. Even had her picture in the newspaper. She was a bookworm, always reading and learning. She was also in the Marine Corps Reserve. Claudette was very conscientious and correct about the military, a reflection of her strict upbringing. To me, though, her uniform only made her look sexier.

But Claudette's sexiness wasn't doing me any good. And to make matters worse, she'd met someone else, a guy named Raleigh Hall.

I was sixteen; Raleigh was twenty. I was a high school kid; Raleigh was an army man. And oh man, jealousy spread over me like a torrid fever! I was afraid of being shot down, even after Raleigh went off to Germany. He was a soldier and I was a nobody. He was writing her twice a week, and soon I learned he was asking her to marry him, and, Lord, if she did, I'd die. This was the girl of my dreams, and suddenly it looked like my dream was turning into a nightmare. Soon she'd be gone.

"You like this guy, don't you?" I'd ask.

"He's nice," she'd answer. "Extremely nice."

And sometimes I'd see his picture around her house, and sometimes I'd see her reading his letters, and sometimes I'd go off in the Hawk riding alone, scared of losing her, and sometimes I'd go home and slam my fist in my pillow, and sometimes I'd cry myself to sleep, 'cause I loved Claudette, no matter what else was happening, I loved that girl till it hurt.

I couldn't escape the obsession. I was upset around graduation time 'cause I'd invited someone else—not Claudette —to the prom. At the last minute I changed my mind. I had to take Claudette. I told Big Sister.

"You can't do that, Smokey."

"I'm doing it," I insisted.

"That other girl's already bought a dress."

"Don't care."

"Well, I do, and so does she."

"I'm crazy about Claudette."

"And you'll be even crazier when I don't let you out of this house for a month. You'll take the girl you asked—and that's final."

Big Sister was my mama, and I minded.

And I cried, and I dreamt about Claudette. Three of my closest pals—Ollie Jones, Sackhead Saxton, Tim Horn—saw me suffering.

"Go tell Claudette you'll stop seeing other chicks," they urged me. "Tell her you love her."

"I told her," I said, "but it ain't doing me no good. This Raleigh's got a spell on her."

To break the spell and change my mood, I got stoned at our graduation picnic. Me and the guys smoked a bunch of black gungi dope. But that only made things wilder and weirder. Tore me up so bad that, watching my basketball colleague drink from a water fountain—six-foot-five-inch George Blackman—I swore he was turning into a giraffe. Didn't touch weed again for another two years.

Meanwhile, a force was moving me in a different direction. It was a musical force, but I believe it was also a spiritual force. I didn't know it, but I was about to meet my destiny.

PART TWO

The Struggle

The Big Meeting

I graduated from Northern High School in June 1957. Rather than start Highland Park Junior College in September, I decided to take a break and not begin till January. The big meeting came in August.

Despite my insecurity about Claudette, things were happening. The Hawk, even with its unreliable brakes, was taking me where I needed to go. The Matadors were rehearsing—playing a few hops and staying sharp—when a cat named Harold, Ronnie White's cousin, gave us the word.

"Jackie Wilson's people are looking for talent," he clued us. "They're auditioning acts."

Wow!

But just as we went into high gear, Sonny went into the Army.

"How can you do this to us, man?" I argued. "We need five voices."

"And I need to get away," he said. He got his parents' permission, and, just like that, Sonny was gone.

How we gonna sing for Jackie's people?

Claudette! I thought to myself.

Claudette was always on my mind, but this time for musical, not romantic, reasons. Claudette had been at our rehearsals. Claudette had been singing with the Matadorettes. Claudette knew our stuff. Why not have Claudette take her brother's place?

Claudette agreed, and we were thrilled.

With me singing lead, our background blend was set: Claudette on top, Bobby's tenor under her, Ronnie's baritone and, at the bottom, Pete's bass.

We'd usually sing outside songs at parties—stuff being played on the radio—but for the audition we decided to do eight songs that I'd written. We were sure that'd make more of an impression. We were wrong.

Day of the big meeting arrives.

We're clean-shaven, we're processed and primped; Claudette looks like a little doll. We're sharp. We're nervous. We're ready. We get to the office, somewhere in midtown Detroit, and we see three guys in the room.

The first is Nat Tarnopol, Jackie's manager; the second is Jackie's music man, Alonzo Tucker, who does all the talking; the third is some short guy our age who sits in the corner and doesn't open his mouth.

"Okay, kids," says Alonzo. "Show us what you got."

We clear our throats, I give a downbeat, and we start singing. Before we get through our program, though, Alonzo lifts his hand.

"That's enough," he says. "I see what you got and it ain't gonna work. You're not bad, but you got the same setup as the Platters, and who needs another Platters when the Platters are already out there? If I were you, I'd do more of a Mickey and Sylvia type thing. Know what I'm saying? Let the girl sing lead with one of the guys. So go home and work that up and give me a call next time we're in town. See ya."

Just like that, it was all over.

Dejected, downhearted, we left the room and were moping down the hallway when the little guy who'd been sitting in the corner came after us.

"Hey, man," he said.

I turned around and looked at him. He was a street dude, short and plainly dressed.

"Yeah?" I asked.

"Who wrote those tunes you were singing?"

"Me."

"Even that one about your mama, the one where you're talkin' 'bout Samson and Delilah."

" 'My Mama Done Tole Me.' Yeah, that's my song."

"That's a pretty good song, man."

"Well, thanks."

"Some of the other songs wandered, but that one hung together."

"You work for Jackie?"

"No, I'm a songwriter, I'm Berry Gordy."

You're Berry Gordy!" Soon as I heard the name, I got excited. I'd always read songwriters' credits on records—always wanted to know who created the shit—and Berry Gordy had written some of Jackie's biggest hits, like "Reet Petite." Couldn't believe it was Berry Gordy, though, 'cause he looked so young. His boyish face hid the fact that he was eleven years older than me.

"Can we talk for a minute?" he asked. "There's a piano in that room over there."

Before we went off by ourselves, I whispered to the cats

and Claudette, "That's Berry Gordy, and I think he's interested in us."

He was.

"Look, man," he said when we were alone in this tiny room, "I don't care what Tucker says. I think your group's all right. How many songs you written?"

"About a hundred."

"A hundred!" He started chuckling.

I took out my trusty Big Ten notebook and showed him. Hell, I'd been writing songs since I popped out of Mama's womb.

"Well, show me your best ones," he said.

As I sang them he pointed out how they were mostly formless. I'd start on one subject, then move to another. That's what he meant by "wandering."

"Your lyrics rhyme up real good, man, but songs are more than rhymes. Songs need a beginning, middle and end. Like a story."

No one had shown me this before.

"You guys out of school?" he asked.

"Yeah, man, we've all graduated."

"Good. Now I'd like to hear you sing something they're playing on the radio. You name it."

"How 'bout Frankie Lymon's 'I'm Not a Know-It-All'?" I asked.

"Fine," he said. "I know that one."

Gordy played piano and I sang, and when I was through, he looked up and smiled, assuring me, as if we'd been friends for years. "I like your voice, man. I really do. It's different. There's no other voice like it out there."

"Thanks."

"I'd like to work with your group. I think I can help you."

"That's great, that's fantastic."

"But right now I gotta catch up with Jackie. Got another tune for him."

"What's it called?"

" 'Lonely Teardrops.' "

Before we left the little room, we exchanged numbers. And when we went out into the hallway, who should be walking towards us but Jackie himself, super-slick in white pants and billowy black silk shirt. His shiny piled-high process looked sculpted. Holy shit! I was blown away!

Both boxers, Berry and Jackie started a mock match, throwing fake punches that never landed, each declaring a knockout. After being introduced to me and my partners, the soul star made a beeline for Claudette.

"Oooo-weeeee!" he cried. "Ain't she a fine thing! Turn 'round, baby," he urged, gently lifting her hand over her head and watching her do a pirouette. Impressed with her lines, Jackie whistled while Claudette blushed, embarrassed and flattered at the same time.

Meanwhile, my head was swimming, my heart flopping like a flounder. So much had happened so quickly—rejection, acceptance, discouragement, encouragement—I wasn't sure where we were headed.

It didn't matter, though, 'cause for the first time someone serious, a dude named Berry Gordy, said he heard something he liked.

Miracles

Let me tell you about my partners:

Ronnie White was small and wiry, a cat heavy into jazz. He dug Cal Tjader and Horace Silver. In fact, he introduced me to modern jazz, and I loved it, loved the percussive flavorings of Max Roach, loved Clifford Brown's rich and tender tone on trumpet. Ronnie favored Ivy League clothes, little thin ties and tweedy sport coats. He was the first dude I knew to wear pants without cuffs. He liked giving off an air of sophistication. He was intellectual, he was street, and also funny as hell.

We called Pete Moore "Pee Wee" 'cause he was short and stocky. Pete idolized the gamers—the pimps and pool sharks—but he wasn't like that. He had a good heart, and excelled at sports. He'd play us at pool with one hand and kick our ass. That wasn't easy since, after we turned sixteen, we *lived* in the pool hall. Pete was also a walking sports almanac. He had his women, but he wasn't as girl aggressive as me and Ronnie.

Bobby Rogers, though, was the biggest playboy. He was the biggest at everything except taking shit seriously. Bobby was lighthearted and life-loving. He always wanted the biggest houses and the biggest cars. He was a genius mechanic and a great interior decorator, the kind of guy who built everything with his own hands. Aside from Claudette, Bobby was our best dancer.

All the cats had quick wit, which is one of the reasons our thing was tight. We liked laughing together, we liked singing together—we even liked rehearsing.

That's just what we were doing the day after we met Berry, honing down our harmonies, with me revising my tunes according to Gordy's guidelines.

During the break, Claudette pulled me aside.

"That Berry guy called me," she said.

"What! What'd he want?"

"He asked me out."

My head started spinning in confusion. "What'd you tell him?"

"No."

"Just like that?"

"I told him I was your girlfriend."

"Oh wow!" She'd never said that before. "And what'd he say?"

"He apologized."

I was too flabbergasted to speak. Only later that night could I tell Claudette what was on my mind.

We'd gone to Belle Isle, an enormous woodsy park in the middle of the Detroit River where guys had picnics during the day and wooed their women at night.

It was one of those summer evenings. You could see the reflections of the city lights shimmering on the water. The air was still. Downriver, smoke from the auto plants floated up into a star-filled sky. Fireflies darted here and there. Crickets hummed, and Claudette, bathed in moonlight, leaned back into my arms.

"Smokey," she confessed, "when you guys were rehearsing, sometimes the girls would peep in on you."

"That so?"

"And once," she went on, "you were singing with your shirt off and the other girls started laughing about how skinny you looked. That got me mad. I told them to shush. I said you didn't look skinny. To me you looked handsome."

"Oh, baby," I said, kissing her lips, "I love you so much. I want you to be my girl."

"Your only girl?"

"I'll give up the others," I promised. "They don't mean anything to me. I swear I'll never see them again."

This time she lifted her mouth towards mine. "I love you, Smokey," she said, her words warming my heart. "I've loved you a long while."

"What about Raleigh?"

"Raleigh's a nice guy. I like him but I don't love him, not the way I love you, Smokey."

"Will you write him and tell him that?"

"I'll write him tomorrow."

"Claudette," I said, kissing her earlobes, her cheeks, her neck, her beautiful mouth, "I'm so happy I could sing."

We stayed there for another hour, locked in each other's arms, promising to be true, promising that she was mine and I was hers and that our love would always stay young.

That night I couldn't fall asleep. I felt thrilled by the promise of the future. Finally, Claudette had agreed to be my girl; finally, my group was getting somewhere. My life was blossoming like a beautiful flower. I was going to college at the end of the year, but, in the back of my mind, I could already feel myself going somewhere else.

Berry Gordy was street, but he was no jitterbug; he wasn't fly, wasn't the kind of cat who strolled with the limp walk. In the past he'd done lots of shit. He'd come out of the same gang era as Jackie Wilson. He'd done his share of fighting, some of it in a ring. He'd paid his dues working the auto plants. He'd opened a jazz record shop that flopped, been married to a lady named Thelma, had three kids, and now was divorced. Had another lady named Raynoma.

When I met him he didn't have money, but he had direction. Working with his partner, Billy Davis, who wrote as "Tyran Carlo," their hits for Jackie didn't generate much cash. In those days writers' royalties were a joke. Mainly, Berry was searching—for songs, talent, a way to get over, a way to get paid. He was a warmhearted cat. He had a knack for handling people, a certain low-key charm, a charisma. He had the smarts to figure out the way the business world was working—or not working—and he had the balls to go after what he wanted.

"I want to manage you guys," he told me straight-off.

"Go ahead, man," I said, knowing no one else had shown interest. "Tell us what you want to do."

At first he got us little gigs. He couldn't give us any money, so we bought our own blue suits, which didn't quite match. Claudette was wearing a white dress with little red flowers.

It wasn't easy. Berry was there, for instance, while we were singing at a dive bar in a basement in Pontiac when dudes got to fighting. They started slashing and we started running, but there was only one way out—this small stairwell. Somehow we squeezed our way up, scared shitless that the razor blades were gonna slice us. Finally, when we made it outside to the Hawk, everyone was exhausted and pissed. Especially at Berry.

On the way back to Detroit, my partners were ragging Berry, running down their beefs in no uncertain terms.

"A real manager wouldn't book us into no jive-ass joint like that."

"Ain't managers supposed to supply outfits for the singers?"

"I think they usually do," I piped up, knuckling in to the peer pressure.

Like he often does, Berry kept quiet.

It was a sad night, and when I dropped everyone off and started home, I couldn't live with myself. I turned the Hawk around and headed back to Berry's place.

"Look, man," I said, "I gotta talk to you."

He was as depressed as me. "What's on your mind?"

"I feel terrible, man. I was bad-mouthing you with the rest of the cats, even though I know goddamn well that you don't have a dime and you're doing this 'cause you really believe in us. I just came to apologize."

His face lit up. "I'm glad you came back, Smokey. You don't know how glad. I was sitting up here feeling like shit, 'specially the way you were agreeing with the other guys. See, I like you so much, man, and I was feeling like you were turning against me. That hurt. I got big plans for you, Smoke. I know we're going to make it. And your coming back here tonight shows me a lot, shows that you really care about me."

We must have talked all night, discussing everything, even how he had hit on Claudette.

"Out of all the cats," said Berry, "she had to say that *you* were her boyfriend. Oh man, I hated hearing that!"

We laughed and laid out on the floor, our heads against

the couch, him telling me about his life, me telling him about mine, two guys scheming and dreaming about things getting better.

"It's gonna happen," he predicted, speaking with such gritty determination that, for the first time, I became a believer myself. At the very least, I knew I'd made a friend.

It happened while I was watching *American Bandstand* on TV. The Silhouettes were singing "Get a Job," number-one song in the world, when it hit me like a bolt of lightning:

Get a job?

Got a job!

Why not write an answer song called "Got a Job"?

I whipped out my Big Ten notebook and started scribbling like crazy. In a few minutes I had the sucker written. The Hawk wasn't running, so I caught the bus over to Berry's, busting in on him, talkin' 'bout, "This is it! I got it!"

"Got what?"

" 'Got a Job.' "

"What's that?"

"Our first hit."

And it was.

Berry helped whip it into form, the group started some serious rehearsing and we cut it over at United Sound in the early part of November 1957. Flip side was "Mama Done Tole Me."

There were no dub-ins or do-overs. In those mono days everything happened at once—the playing, singing and mixing. I'd never been with a producer before. Didn't even know what a producer did. Watching Berry like a hawk, learning all I could, I saw that he was on top of his shit, a perfectionist who pruned the tune till he got an overall dynamite sound.

"You gonna have to change your name," he said afterwards. "The Matadors sounds a little jive."

Everyone thought of a name, scribbled it on a piece of paper and threw it in a hat. By chance we picked my choice.

"Miracles," said Berry, mulling it over. "I like the sound of that. I like the attitude. Yeah, y'all are Miracles."

$3.19

It's January and I'm sitting in freshman English, trying to concentrate on nouns and verbs. It's my first semester at Highland Park Junior College and I should be excited about my schoolwork. The problem is this tiny transistor speaker plugged in my ear. I won't take it out. I can't. I'm listening to Frantic Ernie Durham on WJLB, hoping to hear the Miracles singing "Got a Job," which Berry had sold to End Records. Me and my partners have already listened to it four hundred consecutive times at home, but I've never heard it on the radio. *Please, Frantic Ernie, please play my song!* There's news about Russian sputniks flying around space, there's the hockey scores and finally music comes back on. Ernie plays "Rockin' Robin," he plays "Sweet Little Sixteen" and then— I can't believe it!—he plays us! When "Got a Job" comes on, I start hollering—man, I can't control myself!—and everyone in class thinks I'm nuts. College isn't working. College isn't me. Need to talk to Big Sister, need to talk to Five, but I'm worried what they'll think.

"I wouldn't worry, boy," Daddy made clear. "I've already lived my life. Yours is ahead of you. You young. You got time. If this music thing don't work out, you can always go back to college."

"You made a record," said Big Sister. "You been singing your whole life. Why not try? If it's my blessing you want, you got it."

My dire fear of disappointing my family disappeared in two quick conversations. Daddy and Gerry touched me by supporting my desire. They saw my love of music as genuine and deep, and did nothing to distract me.

My college career was over practically before it began. I was free to follow my heart.

My heart led to Berry's house. Now I was hanging with him hot and heavy, an eager student leaning on a willing teacher. When "Got a Job" started selling, we were ecstatic. Not only were we vibing good personally, but our professional rapport was turning profits. Or so we thought.

We recorded another song called "Money"—not to be confused with a later Motown hit, "Money (That's What I Want)"—with "I Cry" on the flip side, also for the End label.

For these first four sides—and this includes producer's fee, publishing income, writers' and artists' royalties—Berry got a check for $3.19. And keep in mind, "Got a Job" was something of a hit.

"Shit, man," I said to Berry. "This is sure some funky business."

But rather than get down, Berry got up. He took the $3.19 check and framed it.

"We're going to remember this motherfucker," he said, " 'cause I don't intend to let it happen again."

*　　　*　　　*

In the beginning there were six employees—Berry, his second wife Raynoma, Brian Holland (whose singing brother Eddie had been with Berry earlier), Janie Bradford and Robert Bateman, great bass singer and later an engineer.

We'd all meet over at Berry's apartment on Gladstone. Ray was in charge. She was this pretty petite fiery lady—very smart and very behind Berry. She taught us new chords and simple ways to structure songs.

After that $3.19 check, Berry saw that control was the key. He borrowed a little bread from his family and started his own small label, started going for control.

"You think Motown's a name that'll catch on?" he asked.

"It's cute," I said. "Why not try?"

First Motown release was on Marv Johnson, a strong, soulful, local singer. Tune was "Come to Me," and me and Berry were nearly killed going to get it:

Dead of winter, 1958, Berry Gordy behind the wheel. Berry ain't the world's greatest driver, but today he won't be distracted; today he's gotta get where he's going. I'm going nuts with nervousness 'cause I'm riding shotgun and the road's a sheet of glass. The world's turned to snow and ice. We're trucking fifty miles over to Owosso, Michigan, to pick up the actual 45s of "Come to Me" to deliver to record shops and radio stations back in Detroit.

We're slipping and sliding, avoiding crashes by the skin of our teeth, when suddenly a truck swerves towards us and we wind up in a ditch.

"What now?" I ask Berry.

"We need to get those records, man."

It takes a bulldozer to put us back on the road.

We pick up the goods and pile 'em in the trunk. On the way back, though, the road's worse, the storm's howling and here comes another truck slipping past a stop sign and aiming for our ass. Another quick swerve, another fall into another ditch. Another bulldozer, another thirty miles until we finally arrive home—we will *not* be stopped—with the new Marv Johnson single.

Damn if that sucker didn't hit all over the country!

Problem, though, is that we still weren't set up for national sales. So Berry, still learning the ropes, bought himself a new suit, new tie and flew to New York, where he inked a distribution deal with United Artists. To get the contract, however, he signed over Marv. Now Marvin was a UA artist. Berry kept producing his hits—"Merry Go Round," "I Love the Way You Love" and "You Got What It Takes"—but they were all on United Artists.

Berry was still missing the key; the key was still control.

The key was also the Gordy family. When Berry first took me around to their place on Farnsworth and St. Antoine, close to downtown Detroit, I saw how they lived on top of a printing place run by sister Esther and brother Fuller. Everyone in this family was doing something, doing it intensely, and doing it well.

They took me in like I was one of their own.

My own family was and is close. But I'd never seen anything like the Gordys—four sisters and four brothers who made it clear to their lovers and spouses and anyone else that their family came first. The Gordys took care of business, but mainly they took care of each other.

Mother Gordy was political, strong-minded, smart and independent. Pops Gordy was the spiritual spine keeping everyone straight. He was beautiful. When he shook your hand, you felt it; he was a brick mason, tough but tender, a cat who loved the Lord. In good times and bad, Berry went to Pops with his problems.

I loved all these people. They were both down-home and determined. Berry's sisters were especially hip. As years went on Anna would teach me about the real world. Gwen was also my baby, as close as a sister. Loucye was a sweetheart, and a strong-minded businesslady to boot. Esther, married to a prominent state legislator, was brilliant; she became my manager. Berry's brothers—George, Robert and Fuller—became my brothers.

At seventeen, a vulnerable turning point in my life, I was surrounded by this mightily motivated family. I was accepted. I was adopted. I was blessed to benefit from their desire to succeed.

I'd need all those blessings. And I'd need a lot more. I saw the glamour of show business, but I didn't see the heartache and humiliation. Those things were waiting for me, looming just ahead.

Bad Girl

I'm talking to the Hawk.

"Look at that fine thing over there," I say as we cruise down Woodward Avenue in Detroit. "Ain't she something?"

"Hmmm," answers the Hawk, humming right along.

"But, man, lemme tell you, I can't get Claudette off my mind. She's still a virgin, and it's driving me crazy. It's getting harder and harder to break from those clinches. And I'm hearing her body saying the same thing. If we went all the way, man, she wouldn't be a bad girl. See, that's what I'm trying to explain to her."

"Hmmm," the Hawk keeps humming.

"But her parents are strict. They got her believing only bad girls give it up before getting married. You and I know that's jive. Only bad thing she could do would be to leave me. She ain't no bad girl. Bad girl. Hey, that's catchy, ain't it? What about a tune called 'Bad Girl'? That could be something, couldn't it?"

Pulled over to the curb, whipped out my trusty Big Ten and started writing "Bad Girl." Words started flowing, and I also heard a little melody. Because I know the keyboard, when melodies come to me I jot down the letters of the notes, then make arrows indicating if I'm going up or down. Crude but effective.

"A little crude," Berry said to me the next day when I ran over to his house with the tune, "but I think we can fix it."

At first that hurt my feelings. Hell, I'd been up all night with the song running 'round my head. Wasn't even able to concentrate on my date with Claudette. I was half convinced the tune was perfect. But Berry was enthusiastic, he fell in love with the concept, and when he went to the piano and started editing and expanding, I saw again that his song sense was more sophisticated than mine. It was exciting to see Berry when he smelled a hit. The cat would start working like a beaver.

"Bad Girl" was done in the doo-wop vein. In some sense the tune marked the end of the Miracles' doo-wop period and the start of our national career. It was our first national hit.

When it broke big, though, Berry still didn't have a coast-to-coast sales link. So he sold distribution rights to Chess, the famous blues label out of Chicago.

We were going out of our minds, overjoyed over a success we never imagined would have come so quickly.

"You better get out on the road," said Berry.

And naturally, because he was a manager and mentor, we listened to him; we went out there.

And died the death of a lonely lobster in boiling water.

New York City, 1958, Apollo Theater, our first big-time gig.

The Apollo was the acid test, the ultimate proving ground of soul singers, dancers and comics. If that hard-ass audience didn't like you, they'd let you know.

Mama.

Smokey, Daddy and Mama.

I'm fourteen months, niece Sylvia is two.

Big Sister Gerry.

Uncle Claude holding me on his right knee and Sylvia on his left, with a neighbor in the middle.

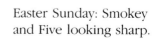

Easter Sunday: Smokey and Five looking sharp.

SCHOLARSHIP

Scholarship is the child's achievement in the subjects taught in the school. Both ability and interest are important. Satisfactory progress is marked **S**. Unsatisfactory work is marked **U**. An unusually high quality of work is marked **E** for excellent.

SUBJECTS	First Report	Second Report	Third Report
Arithmetic	E	E	E
Art	E	E	E
Elementary Science	S	S	S
English			
General Language			
General Science			
Handwriting			
Health Education	S	E	S
Home Economics			
Industrial Arts			
Literature	E	E	E
Music	S	S	S
Reading	E	E	E
Social Studies	E	E	E
Spelling	E	E	E
Auditorium	S	E	E

Got almost all "excellents," but what happened in music?

The neighborhood dudes. *From left:* Vaughn Jones, Smokey, Feebee Williams, Sackhead Saxton.

The Five Chimes, 1954. Clarence "Humble" Dawson, Pete "Peewee" Moore, Ronnie "Whitey" White, Smokey and James "Rat" Grice.

Claudette's high school graduation, 1954.

Smokey's high school graduation, 1957.

Smokey and Claudette, young and in love.

With Pete at my wedding ... we finally found the ring.

Claudette Rogers To Sing
Forever With Wm. Robinson

Two "Miracles" were united in holy matrimony on Saturday, Nov. 7, at the Warren Avenue Baptist church, with Rev. William R. Matthews officiating at the impressive afternoon ceremonies.

Miss Claudette A. Rogers, an only female member of the "Miracles" quintet, and William Robinson, Jr., were the couple whose romance bud and saw maturity whe performed ferem

copen, fashioned into silk taffeta in short moderately full skirts with a square back coming to a "V" with box pleats; the neckline was round for the neat bodice with cap sleeves. Their headwear were matching bands, and they carried nosegays of lemon yellow by mums with ribbons. of honor was

Ringo, Joyce Edwards, Fannie Williams, Sharon Burston, Lillie Brown, Rebecca Ringo and Linda Marable.

Among the special guests were celebrities Jackie Wilson, Larry D i x o n, the Raybus Voices, the Satin Tones, Barett

and Bill and the other "Miracles."

The bride and groom as members of the quintet are planning a short undisclosed honeymoon and continuing it in Baltimore, Md., when the group again goes on tour there

Here's how the papers handled it . . .

The bride and groom, 1959.

Primitive poster.

Primitive product.

Berry in the beginning.

The Isley Brothers, backstage in 1960. *From left*: Kelly, Elaine Jasper Isley (Rudy's wife), Rudy and Ronnie.

Not the Everly Brothers.

The first supersmash.

Thank you, Claudette.

Life on the road in the early sixties. *From left*: Ronnie White, Bobby Rogers, Pete Moore, Claudette and Smokey.

We died during our first Apollo gig, but Claudette was still smiling.

Miracles overhead. *From left, above* Smokey: Bobby, Claudette, Ronnie and Pete.

Marvin Gaye and Claudette.

Moving into our first house, 19357 Santa Barbara, in December 1962.

From left: Claudette, Smokey, Annette Butler, Jerry Butler and Ruth Brown.

From left:
Robert Gordy,
Anna Gordy Gaye,
Claudette and
Smokey.

From left: Georgeanna Dobbins (a Marvelette),
Claudette, Florence Ballard (a Supreme), Mary Wells
and Wanda Young (a Marvelette).

"Sing it, Smokey!" Claudette performs
down South, 1962.

Check the stingy brim.

We were billed with
the best.

Marvin Gaye in 1962.
Seated next to him is
Ronnie White.

Christmas with the Miracles (Pete was in the army), 1962.

We weren't ready. Weren't nearly ready. We had our one little hit, but our routine was still raggedy. Didn't even have real arrangements for the house band.

Making matters worse, we were on the Ray Charles show. He was an idol of mine and, at the time, the hottest thing going. His "What'd I Say" was burning up the charts.

We got backstage and first thing Honi Coles, theater manager and legendary hoofer, wanted to see were the charts for the band.

I pulled out these pathetic-looking chord sheets with a few notes scribbled for the vocals. We didn't have any music for the band.

"What the hell is this?" hollered Honi. "The band can't play this crap."

"Hey, man," said another, deeper voice. "These cats are just getting started. They probably don't know nothing about charts."

I looked up and gulped. It was Ray Charles, speaking on our behalf. Couldn't believe it. He spoke with tremendous authority and, adding to my amazement, he looked just like Daddy Five.

"Which of you guys can play the song for me?" asked Brother Ray.

"I suppose I can," I mumbled meekly.

"Well, come over here, man, and run it down."

Me and Ray went over to the piano, where, nervously, I showed him our tunes. Off the top of his head, he called out the notes to each individual musician. Within minutes he had worked out these beautifully tight charts, punchy as a hard-hitting prizefighter.

"How can I ever thank you, Mr. Charles?"

"Forget it."

But I never have, and never will.

Never will forget that week 'cause, in spite of Ray's arrangements, we bombed.

We were pitiful and I was petrified. I memorized the back wall of the Apollo perfectly—every crack and paint blemish. I was too freaked to look at the audience. Our dancing was jerky. Our stage presence was so wobbly, the owner, Mr. Schiffman, wanted his bread back.

"How the hell can you send these kids out here," he screamed over the phone at Berry, "when they're still amateurs! I want a refund on that $750 I paid them."

He didn't get it, 'cause that $750—for all five of us—didn't even cover expenses. Berry had to wire us more bread.

The whole thing was a disaster.

We came home, our tail between our legs, our ass whipped, our spirit nearly broken.

"It's about paying dues," said Berry. "Meanwhile, you need practice. You gotta work this shit till you get it right."

I sighed, and couldn't help but agree. After all, didn't Mama always say the same thing? "Learn from the best, improve on the best, be the best."

"We best head over to Belmont," I told Claudette and the boys. "We got work to do."

To us the Apollo was a bitter pill to swallow, but to the kids in the neighborhood we were heroes. After all, we'd made three records. You could hear us on the radio.

One little neighbor was especially interested in our success. I knew her 'cause her folks had rented a flat from Mrs. Wiggins, right down the street, the woman who gave me a job at her Two Sisters Unique store. Her tenants were the Ross family.

Their kids were younger than me—three boys and three girls—but the middle girl, Diane, was tight with my niece Sharon. And it was Diane who loved to hang around and watch us—the Chimes, the Matadors and finally the Miracles—singing and rehearsing.

She was shy about it, but always persistent. If we were practicing in the basement, she'd be listening on the staircase. If we were in the living room, she'd be on the front porch. She was a fan, a music lover, and sometimes Big Sister would hear her sing.

"You got a cute voice, honey," she'd say.

"I love singing," Diane couldn't deny, "but I'm not good enough to be a real singer."

I always noticed her 'cause she was pretty and perky and pushy, pushing herself to do better—studying clothes design and cosmetics, smart enough to get into Cass Tech like my sister Rose Ella had done years before.

After we had our first records out, Diane surprised me.

I hadn't seen her since her family moved from Belmont to the Brewster housing project.

"Smokey!" she said, always sparky and spunky. "I've been hearing your records. I'm so proud of you, and I can't wait for you to hear our group."

"You have a group, Diane?"

"The Primettes. Will you listen to us? Will you introduce us to Berry Gordy?"

"Well, we're about to go back out on the road at the end of the week."

"Then we'll come over tomorrow night."

She did. Brought Mary Wilson, Florence Ballard and Barbara Martin along with her. Four foxes. Sexy and stylishly dressed. Fact is, they looked better than they sang. They weren't bad, just not polished.

Their guitarist, though, was a monster, smoothest I'd ever heard. I mean, this cat made magic with his fingers. Had a gentle touch, an easy-wristed riffin' approach, sweet, swinging and steady as a rock. I flipped. His personality was as cool as his playing—laid back, funny in a quiet way, the kind of dude who was smarter than he let on.

"Tell you what, girls," I proposed, eager to close a deal, still feeling the fresh pain of our Apollo date, "I think we can help each other. We need a musician to rehearse and tour with us. Your guitarist might be the guy. If he's willing, I'd like to use him for a while. Then when we get off tour, I promise I'll set up something for you with Berry. What do you say?"

Enthusiastically, they said yes.

Two weeks later we were at the Arena in Cleveland, playing on a bill with Jackie Wilson and Little Willie John. Back then, Little Willie, one of the best singers of all time, had the baddest band in the land, the Upsetters.

We were still raw, still uncertain and awkward, but at least we had our own guitarist. That week Marv Tarplin stood onstage behind me. Ever since then—it's over thirty years now—I've never played onstage without him.

I was lucky. I caught the last leg of vaudeville. I played the chitlin circuit with comics, dogs and one-legged dancers. I caught people like Red Foxx, Moms Mabley, Nipsey Russell and Slappy White. We played with the blues legends, Jimmy Reed and John Lee Hooker, Lightnin' Hopkins and Howlin' Wolf. We saw one era end and another begin. It was a privilege, a blessing, a beautiful chapter in the history of black show business. It was also bizarre. And brutal, especially down South, where you couldn't get a hotel for the color of your skin and the accommodations weren't fit for a dog. Those were the dues.

I was also lucky 'cause I didn't face this alone. I had my partners, the Miracles. I was not only close to my pals, but next to the woman I was growing to love more every day.

This was the time—a crazy time of hopping, flopping, thriving, striving and driving—when I decided to pop the question.

"*I Do*"

"This doesn't make sense," I said softly to Claudette as I took my shift driving down the dark highway. Four hours before we'd played Philadelphia. Now we were riding through heavy night rain, heading home. We were exhausted.

Claudette was my copilot, helping me stay awake, while the other cats slept in the back of a funky old VW minibus Berry had bought us.

"What doesn't make sense, Smoke?"

"Our life."

"I thought you loved it. I thought you were happy the way things are going."

"Are you?" I asked.

"I'm happy if you're happy. We're recording, we're performing, we're getting a little better each night."

Suddenly, a diesel truck, speeding in the opposite direction, nearly blew us away. Our tiny minibus could barely hold the road.

We caught our breath, pushed the fear back down our throats and carried on the conversation.

"What are you trying to say, Smoke?"

"Your folks aren't thrilled about you traveling 'round with all these single guys."

"They trust me."

"Well, I'm not thrilled about it."

"You firing me?" she joked.

"I'm trying to tell you something."

"Then say it."

"It's not easy."

"You aren't pregnant, are you, Smokey?"

"Stop kidding around, Claudette, this is serious."

"I want to hear the words."

"Will you ..." I tried, but I couldn't say the rest. I was nervous, unsure, off balance. In the distance bolts of lightning electrified the midnight sky. A clap of thunder punctured the silence.

"Will I *what*?" Claudette wanted to know.

"Look, baby," I blurted out, "we gotta get married."

"Ain't that sweet!" hollered the merry band of Miracles from the back seat. The thunder had awakened them.

"It *is* sweet," Claudette assured them and me, snuggling up close and kissing me on the cheek. "And I will. Soon as you can convince my mama and daddy."

Daddy Rogers was willing, he said, long as I could feed Claudette.

"Claudette," he joked, "is one hell of an eater."

Mama Rogers was more reluctant, seeing that I didn't have a steady job. But she finally came round.

"I've watched you grow up, Smokey," she said. "I've seen how much you love her."

Now I had my mama, Big Sister, to worry about.

When I got home the house was jammed. Kids running 'round everywhere.

"We got to have a private talk," I told Gerry.

"There's no place private in this house 'cept the bathroom."

"Then let's talk there."

Crowded inside the bathroom, leaning against the tub, I said, "I've got something serious to discuss, Big Sister."

"You and Claudette in trouble?"

"No, we're in love."

"I know that. You want to marry her, don't you?"

"You think I'm crazy?"

"I think you're in love. I just worry about your finances. How much you making?"

"Royalties aren't coming in yet. After expenses, we aren't making anything on the road. And my salary from Motown is only five dollars a week."

"Where do you and Claudette plan to live?"

"I don't know."

"Well, I do."

"Where?"

"Here."

"I couldn't do that to you, Big Sister. We're already over-crowded."

"You and Claudette will live upstairs. There's an empty bedroom in Daddy Five's flat. And you'll eat with us too."

I felt great. You can see why I love her so.

Suddenly there was a loud knock at the door. "Hey!" shouted Sharon. "What's going on in there?"

"We've just solved a problem," Gerry shouted back.

"The problem is that I don't have the ring."

"What!"

"I kid you not, man, I don't have the damn ring!"

This is my best man, Pete Moore, talking to me. We're in the Hawk, a block away from the church, when he realizes he forgot the ring. I U-turn on a dime—tires screeching, rubber burning—race home, grab the gold and speed back to church. We're so late, folks figured I'd flaked out.

Turned out beautiful, though. We said "I do" at the Warren Avenue Baptist Church, where Claudette was raised.

Everyone was at the reception—Berry, the Miracles, even Jackie Wilson. He shocked us all by showing up, fresh from a gig at the Apollo. When he walked through the door, you should've seen the heads turn. Man, he looked sharper than the bridegroom. I didn't care; I was honored that, in such short time, I'd gone from being his fan to his friend. Besides, Jackie was another Dr. Jekyll and Mr. Hyde type. One minute he loved you, the next you were on his shit list. I was glad to be on his good side.

"Watch Jackie," I said to Claudette as he approached our table. "He'll never get past that mirror without stopping."

Sure enough, he stopped at the mirror, checked his smile, fished his fine-toothed comb from his pocket and smoothed out his doo before offering us his best.

No rest. "The test is never over," said Berry. "Y'all need to get back out there and keep pushing 'Bad Girl.' We need air play."

Our honeymoon wasn't much more than a quick night at a hot-sheet motel in Detroit. And not all that hot. See, Claudette and I had sex twice before marrying, and both times were disasters. She was nervous and I was awkward. For Claudette it was more pain than pleasure. Actually, it wasn't till a year after our marriage that we really began enjoying ourselves sexually. The love was always there, but the passion—and freedom to explore it—came later.

The rush of the road came first. A week after our wedding Berry had given me a $3.00 weekly raise, and we were in Philly, the bottom act of a big bill featuring the Coasters, Drifters, Flamingos, Shirelles, Isley Brothers and Jerry Butler.

The Coasters were the headliners—they came on last—but the Isleys were slamming so hard with their smash "Shout," no one could follow 'em. When the promoter decided that the Isleys should close the show, the Coasters coasted off in a huff, leaving town.

Compared to the other acts, the Miracles really weren't stepping. Our dance moves still sucked. The mood of the show made me see how fiercely performers competed. It was ruthless. But in the midst of the battle I was touched—the way Brother Ray had touched me earlier—by an act of kindness and grace.

Enter the Ice Man.

Jerry Butler had been around. He was a great singer and writer, more experienced than me, but, also like me, a newlywed traveling with his wife. That gave us something in common. Jerry was so cool, they called him the Ice Man. Had these bedroom eyes and a deep, silk-and-satin voice.

"Don't take this wrong," he advised me, "but you guys are trying too hard, rushing onstage with all that fanfare. Less is more. You dig? Try walking out there with a slow, cool, cocky strut. Show some confidence. Let me teach you a couple of simple steps, man, a little body language that'll go a long way."

Jerry led and we followed, a free lesson from a beautiful soul who's remained a lifelong friend.

*　　　*　　　*

Back in Detroit things were humming.

Berry was breaking his ass trying to break our records. We'd do anything for a hit. For a minute we even formed a recording group called Ron and Bill, modeled after the Everly Brothers. Ronnie White was "Ron" and I was "Bill," but the duo didn't make any miracles.

After the Miracles' "Bad Girl," our contract was up with Chess. Meanwhile, me and Berry had written "Way Over There." Berry got so excited, he flew us to Chicago to record with strings. The session was rough, but we finally got a good take.

What then?

"Got any ideas?" Berry asked me.

"A big one," I said.

"Shoot."

"Look, we keep recording good tunes, turning them into local hits and then selling our masters to these big-ass companies who never pay. The way you do business, man, you should be selling us coast to coast and cutting out the middleman."

"You believe in me that much?"

"And more. If you can't do this shit, no one can."

"Man, your confidence in me is really inspiring."

"It's time, Berry. I'm telling you, it's time."

And it was.

Hopping and Shopping

Motown was on the move.

Harvey Fuqua, of Harvey and the Moonglows, a master musician, blew into town with a mysterious guy named Marvin Gaye. They started working with Anna Gordy at her small record label.

Anna and Harvey recorded a song, written by Berry and Janie Bradford, on Barrett Strong called "Money (That's What I Want)," an anthem for us all.

By then Berry had decided to go national with sales. Anna asked him to distribute "Money." He did, along with our "Way Over There." Our song did well. But Barrett's "Money" broke the bank, becoming Motown's first coast-to-coast stone smash.

Finally, we were a legit national firm.

We were kicking ass.

"Work with Barrett," Berry asked me. "We've been cutting all these singles. Now albums are starting to happen. I want you to do an album on Barrett."

I'd studied Berry's studio style long enough; it was time to do it alone. Or so I thought.

I wrote a thing called "Shop Around" in a half hour. It

was another mama-done-tole-me ditty. Because Mama really did tell me so much stuff, her wisdom was an inexhaustible well of inspiration.

"What do you think?" I asked the boss.

Berry got excited. "This could be something," he said, heading to the piano to fool with the chords. Forty minutes later we had the song.

"I want you to sing it, Smoke," he insisted.

"It's for Barrett."

"It'll be a hit on the Miracles. Trust me."

I produced and recorded it on the Miracles with a slow, bluesy beat.

Two weeks after the record came out, I was asleep and the phone was ringing off the wall.

"Smoke, what's happening?"

"Berry?" I asked, still in dreamland.

"What's happening, man?" he repeated.

"What could be happening at three in the morning? I'm sleeping."

"Haven't been able to sleep, Smokey. Not tonight. Not last night. Not the night before that. Can't get 'Shop Around' out of my mind."

"It's already in the stores. Forget it."

"Look, Smoke," he said, his voice filled with passion, "I don't want to criticize your production, man, but I got a new idea for rerecording it. I got a different beat, and . . ."

"Good," I said, closing my eyes, "we'll talk about it tomorrow."

"I want to rerecord the sucker tonight."

"That's crazy."

"The musicians are waiting."

"I can't believe this."

"They're already out in the studio."

"You're out of your mind, Berry. It's three in the morning."

"I don't give a shit what time it is. Just wake up Claudette, call the cats and get them over there. I'm telling you, Smoke, I feel it in my gut. This thing can go number one."

An hour later we were at the studio, shaking our heads in wonder. Everyone was in place except for a no-show piano player.

"Leave it to me," said Berry, nearly frantic with enthusiasm, sitting at the keyboard, where he led the session, speeding up the tempo and simplifying the rhythm.

A few weeks later the results were in:

"Shop Around" was a number-one smash, on the white chart as well as the black. This was the song that established Motown and the Miracles and, along with "Money (That's What I Want)," sent the company sailing into orbit. We were flying high.

Were it not for certain folks with their feet on the ground, though, we'd never have taken off.

In the office, Berry's sister Loucye was working the books while sister Esther and Barney Ales were setting up a dynamite sales force, first nationally, then internationally.

Barney was white, the first of many whites to help us in our struggle to succeed. See, our idea was to win, to make hit records while controlling production and sales. That meant we'd need the expertise of people more experienced than us. Our specialty was black music—that's what we knew, that's who we were—but that didn't mean we didn't want the help of everyone. In the early sixties, America was fighting the notion of segregation, and so were we. We wanted and needed an integrated company. Made no apologies about it. Still don't.

Berry, I believe, was hip in another regard. He believed in

women, not just as secretaries, but as executives. His first two vice presidents were women, Raynoma and Loucye. Through the years women played a major role in running the company. His own mama, a powerful world-wise lady, showed him that fencing in females was foolish. Berry was big on letting people prove themselves, based on skill, not sex or color.

Despite the astonishing amount of talent in the history of black music, there'd never been a big-time record company owner who was black. This was the gold Berry was going for; to get it he was smart enough to know that, in many areas, others were smarter than him. Berry was proud but practical—he'd hire anyone who'd help him score.

"You've scored, man." Berry flashed me one of his ear-to-ear smiles. "Look outside."

Sitting at the curb was a brand-new Ford station wagon wrapped up in bright green-and-red ribbons like a Christmas present. "Miracles" was written across a white banner. Later, we emblazoned our individual names on the doors in fire-engine red.

Off the success of "Shop Around," we returned to the Apollo, this time our heads high. That first fearful experience was nothing but an ugly memory. We weren't headliners yet, but we were third from the top. Our dancing was sharper. We were styling and stepping with confidence.

Sometimes I think heaven is stepping out at the Apollo on the heels of a hit. We'd sing our songs, get a standing ovation, go back to the dressing room, only to be called out again and again—even after the other acts were on—to repeat "Shop Around." Sang it three times in one show.

Backstage, it looked like every kid from the audience was

asking us for autographs. Women were lined up on 126th Street, behind our dressing room, throwing flowers at our window. It was wild.

"Ronnie! Bobby! Pete! Claudette! Smokey!"

We couldn't believe they knew us by name, but they did, screaming for us as we ran for the car. What a mistake to put our names on the door! We barely escaped the mob.

Back at the Theresa Hotel, we felt like Harlem royalty. Outside, the record shops sounded like they were waging a Miracles war, one store blasting our songs louder than the other. Back then the shops all had those tinny outdoor speakers. To me, though, the sound was beautiful. They were playing "Shop Around" as well as the flip side, "Who's Loving You." It was our first of many two-sided hits.

All evening I heard those songs, and all night too. Cars drove by, horns honking, fans waving up at our room, our music blaring from their radios. Never been so thrilled. I was too excited to sleep. Seemed like the world was ours.

"Claudette," I asked, "is this all just a dream?"

I turned over to see that her eyes were closed. From outside our window, flashing neon cast a wondrous glow over her beautiful body. I kissed her softly and thanked God for the blessings of my life.

I was sure my life was ending. Had 106-degree temperature. Man, I was shaking like I had malaria. I was delirious. Far too sick to sing.

We were staying at a boardinghouse across the street from the Howard Theater in D.C. Each night, after the last show, Claudette would rush me to the hospital where the doctors would throw me in this huge thing that looked like a laundry basket. They would fill it with ice to bring down my temperature. The crazy contraption saved my life.

Later, they said I was America's first victim of the Asian flu, an honor I could've lived without.

The show, though, had to go on, and the Miracles went on without me, heading south for a grueling tour of fifty-two one-nighters.

Recuperating back in Detroit, I picked up the phone a few weeks later. It was Berry in a jovial mood.

"Hey, man, they're loving you in Georgia."

"What are you talking about?"

"They keep screaming at you."

"I don't get it."

"They don't either. Claudette's singing all your lead parts, and they're hollering at her, 'Sing it, Smokey, sing it!' From the voice on the records," Berry laughed, "they think Smokey's a girl!"

"I think he's a faggot. With a voice like that, he's gotta be a faggot."

I'm in a tailor shop in Philly and this cat's rattling my cage. He's one of these needlers, itching for action. Me, I'm still thinking *sticks and stones*. I ignore him.

"I hate these fairies," the guy continues. "They're taking over the world. Someone needs to teach 'em a lesson."

The man's so determined to fight, he fakes an accident, bumping and knocking me to the ground.

A left hook to his jaw was my measured reply.

We wind up on the street, slugging it out. The passersby get a good show. I wreck the bastard. Feel foolish fighting for my manhood, but, like any other dude, you can only push me so far.

Grand Designs

West Grand Boulevard was the name of the street. Berry had bought a routine, B-flat two-story house on the same strip as a funeral home and beauty shop. We were wedged in between. He and Ray and their newborn son Kerry moved upstairs. Downstairs became headquarters. Kitchen became the control room. Garage became the studio where we'd cut "Way Over There" and "Shop Around." The living room was bookkeeping, the dining room, sales. Berry stuck a funky sign in the front window—"Hitsville, U.S.A."—and we were in business.

The house was the womb for an astounding number of artistic births. That's where we were nourished, where we grew and fought and loved, played and provoked and produced and sang an array of songs that would enter into the lives and souls of millions of people all over the world. At the time we were just local kids trying to get over. And, believe me, it wasn't easy.

Wasn't easy for me in 1962 because that long southern tour—the first Motor Town Revue—was still on and I was still out, recovering from the Asian flu. Claudette was still far away.

*　　　*　　　*

"You sound so far away, Mary," I said, wiping the sleep from my eyes.

"I am. I'm calling from Atlanta."

It was a bitter cold, mid-November midnight in Detroit, and I wondered why Mary Wells was calling me.

Not that I wasn't glad. I had fond feelings for Mary. "Found this soulful-sounding chick," Berry had told me a year earlier, "who I want you to work with." Mary became my pet project. Shy and eager to please the producer, she'd done a wonderful job on her first recording, "Bye Bye Baby." I liked writing for her voice. Liked experimenting with her sound. In fact, I took my love for Harry Belafonte's calypso and gave an island flavor bongo bop to "The One Who Really Loves You." It hit big. So did "You Beat Me to the Punch" and "Two Lovers." Later, I wrote "My Guy," her biggest hit of all.

"What's happening, Mary?"

"Smoke, the guys would kill me if they knew I was calling you."

"Why?"

"Claudette would be even angrier."

"I don't understand, Mary."

"I don't either, Smoke. I don't know why she doesn't tell you."

"Tell me *what*?"

"Look, Smoke, I shouldn't be saying this, but I love Claudette, I really do, she's my roommate and my friend and . . ."

"Tell me, Mary. For God's sake, *tell me!*"

"Claudette's pregnant."

My heart started hammering; my throat went dry. "Is she all right?" was all I could ask.

"No, she's not all right. That's why I'm calling you. She's bleeding, bleeding something awful, and the guys in the group, well, they're not even helping carry her bags. Only James Jamerson, the bass player, he's the only gentleman. I don't think it's right, Smoke, and it's something you needed to know."

"Is Claudette there? Can I talk to her?"

"I'm calling from a pay phone. She's up in the room."

Mary gave me the number and, frantic with fear, I called Claudette.

"Baby, I just talked to Mary and . . ."

"She shouldn't have told you, Smokey. I wanted to surprise you, not worry you."

"I'm surprised, but I'm worried as hell. I want you home, right now. And what about this bleeding?"

"It stopped. I went to a doctor today and he stopped the bleeding. He said I was fine."

"Thank God. That's even more reason to come home, to make sure things stay fine."

"It wouldn't be fair to the guys. Christmas is coming up, and they need the money."

"You need to be home. We're having a baby, and I want you here with me."

"Look, Smokey, Pete's in the Army and you're in the sickbed. That leaves just me, Ronnie and Bobby. The fans won't accept just two Miracles. It wouldn't be right."

"It's not right for you, in your condition, to be on the road."

"Everything will turn out fine, honey, believe me."

"I love you, Boo Boo"—that was my pet name for Claudette—"and I don't want anything to happen to you or our baby."

"I'll be home by Christmas, Doo." She called me Doo 'cause back then I was always running around with my doo-rag on.

"Christmas is a long way off."

"It's sooner than you think."

Sooner than I thought, the phone rang. It was Thanksgiving Day. A week had passed, a week of uneasy sleep and nightly calls to Claudette. Every time the phone rang, I jumped. This was no exception.

"Smokey," said Claudette, her voice quivering. "There's been a terrible accident."

"What happened?" I asked, scared shitless. "Are you all right?"

"It's not me. It's Little Eddie."

"Eddie McFarland, the driver?"

"He was driving Beans Bowles in the station wagon. They were on their way to Miami when they were hit by a truck. Eddie was killed, Smokey, and Beans is in a coma."

Claudette was crying and I was too shook to speak. Eddie was a sweet cat, and Beans, a great baritone saxist, was the tour manager.

"Oh, honey," was all I could say, choking on my own tears, "I want you to come home."

Beans survived, and Claudette finally did come home, only five days before the end of the tour. By then it was mid-December.

At the airport, when she got off the plane, I hardly recognized her. I thought I was seeing a ghost. Down to eighty-nine pounds, the woman was all skin and bones. I didn't want to hug her too hard 'cause she was three months pregnant. She was so thin, I thought she'd break.

"You're the littlest pregnant lady in the land," I told her.

"I'm not showing much, am I?"

"I'm showing you the way home, honey, where I'm not letting you out of my sight."

She kissed me and confessed, "It's been a little rough."

We had a small one-bedroom apartment at Sturtevant and Lawton in the northwest part of Detroit. Nothing fancy. Folks figured I was rich by then, but far from it. Song royalties were slow in coming. Motown was operating on a shoestring. Big money was still years away.

"Now I want to get you big and fat," I told Claudette after I carried her to the bed. "I want you to do nothing but concentrate on being healthy."

The doctor urged her to stay off her feet, and predicted everything would be all right.

We were like two peas in a pod. I stayed close to Claudette, didn't mind bringing her food, didn't want to do anything to upset her. We were both dying to have this baby.

At the beginning of the fifth month a guy came over to show us slides of baby carriages. Claudette and I looked at the pictures, smiling, holding hands, filled with expectancy and joy. When I read a guarantee on the last slide—"In case of a miscarriage, your money will be refunded"—I remember thinking how that could never happen to us.

Two weeks later it happened.

Claudette's water broke. At the hospital they said it was too late. The baby was gone.

We were devastated.

"It's okay, baby," I tried to reassure her, "long as we have each other."

But that sort of pain doesn't disappear quickly or easily. It lingers in the heart, feeds on the mind, erodes the soul. At the same time it brought me and Claudette closer together, even as tongues started wagging, wanting to tear us apart.

Supreme Friendships

I loved Diane Ross. I still do. She was my neighborhood buddy, and she depended on me. She knew I'd be real with her. And so was Berry. He made the girls finish high school before he signed them. Even before that, Diane, never one to be denied, worked as a secretary at the Hitsville office, just to be close to the action.

Diane and I had been close for years. I admired her spunk and her smarts. In fact, when she needed money for cosmetology school, I loaned it to her. I applauded her ambition. I also helped her through her driving test. We celebrated when she got her license, and we celebrated when she graduated Cass Tech. She was a heady mixture of sweetness and aggression. She had drive—that much was clear—and she had charm. In the beginning, though, none of us knew the enormous range of her talent.

In 1962, after Barbara Martin had left the group now known as the Supremes, I recorded some songs on them— "Your Heart Belongs to Me," "Who's Lovin' You"—but nothing happened.

"Is anything *ever* going to happen, Smoke?" Diane would

ask, seeing how Mary Wells and the Miracles were getting hits and she wasn't.

"Eventually talent wins out," I'd tell her. "Problem is, you never know when."

I pleaded for patience. I'd tell her that I liked her voice, though not everyone did. I heard her nasal quality as sexy and unique. With the right tune, I thought, her voice would cut through. None of my tunes on the Supremes, though, hit the charts.

We rehearsed together; we worked late. We developed an intimacy, a genuine love and respect. We enjoyed each other's company.

"The word, Doo, is that you're really enjoying Diane's company," Claudette said to me one day.

"What does that mean?"

"You tell me."

"She's my friend."

"People say she's more."

"People say all kinds of shit. People love to gossip."

"Well, it's getting back to me."

"If the gossip's upsetting you . . ."

"It's upsetting me a lot," Claudette said, plainly and honestly.

I thought about it. The last thing in the world I wanted to do was upset Claudette.

"Would it make you feel better if I didn't see Diane so much?"

"It would."

"Then I'll cool it."

And I did.

*   *   *

Marvin Gaye had lousy feet. He walked gingerly, trying to avoid aggravating his bunions and corns.

"The way you creep around here," I told him one day, "you remind me of an old man. I'm calling you 'Dad.'"

In the early days, Dad, like Diane, liked to hang around, looking for a spot, an opening, an opportunity. He was a versatile musician, a first-rate drummer. That's how I happened to ask him to do a gig with us at the Rockland Palace in New York. He jumped at the chance.

On the way Dad got to talking. He spoke, like he walked, so softly you could hardly hear him. He whispered in a cool kicked-back manner, hiding, I believe, the intensity inside.

"Smoke," he explained, "I got a plan for my solo career."

Dad had a plan for everything.

"See," he said, "when I get out there, don't look for me to be singing no rock 'n' roll."

"What are you going to be singing, Dad?"

"Standards. Love songs. Slow ballads. Like Sinatra. I'm going to be the black Sinatra."

"Tonight," I said, "you're going to be the black drummer for the Miracles. And we're looking for you to kick ass."

"I'm looking for Dad," Ronnie said four hours later when we were about to go onstage. "You seen him?"

No one had seen him. We all started running around the place, searching for Marvin.

Finally, forty minutes later, he turned up.

"I was out buying the gangster," he said, using the street term for pot, "and lost track of time."

He confessed in such a sweet way—sweetness was one of Dad's trademarks—I couldn't stay mad for long.

Around that same time Dad fell madly in love with Anna, one of Berry's sisters. I could dig it 'cause I loved Anna too.

She's good people. She swept Marvin off his feet; I mean, he was bonkers for the lady. He married her, and he also started recording those standards he thought would gain him fame. He was wrong, but stubborn, and his stubbornness, you'll soon see, became the name of his game.

Ronnie White's brother Gerald had a friend. Said he was real musical. Called him amazing. Bugged Ronnie about him until Ronnie heard him. Bugged me until I heard him. Bugged Berry until Berry heard him.

Finally, we all heard him, we dug him and started calling him Baby Ray 'cause he was like a little Ray Charles.

He was a blind whiz kid named Steveland Morris, but Berry, after signing him and finding him tutors, called him Little Stevie Wonder.

He was ten—hyper, bright, brimming with talent. He needed lots of work, but he was willing. He leaped around the studio like a frog, beating the drums, blowing the harmonica, eating up sounds like they were candy.

Within two years he had a big record called "Fingertips." His growth, like Motown's, could hardly be contained. Later his philosophical chatter could be a little long-winded, but I never stopped loving him. Our musical paths would soon meet, complicating my life in ways both wonderful and worrisome.

Meanwhile, even as I was writing, recording, producing, performing and traveling, I always had time for my main man.

When the Cleveland Indians came to town, it was me and Daddy Five at Tiger Stadium. Baseball brought us together.

One summer night was especially muggy. The mosquitoes were out in force. No matter, the grass was green, the lights were bright and Al Kaline and Norm Cash were systematically destroying Cleveland. I couldn't help but get on Daddy's case.

"They need you out there," I'd say.

"They need Satchel Paige," he'd shoot back.

"You're living in the past."

"Boy, you're living on borrowed time. These Indians of mine are about to scalp the stripes off your Tigers."

It turned into a demolition derby for Detroit. By the sixth inning we were ahead 7-0. Daddy doused himself with beer while I went through a couple of boxes of popcorn. I was having a ball, thinking about nothing in particular, when, out of nowhere, a song started running 'round my head. I felt a little melody fluttering in my heart. Words came to mind. Quickly I grabbed a pencil and, on the popcorn box, scribbled lyrics that seemed to fall from heaven:

I will build you a castle with a tower so high
It reaches the moon

I'll gather melodies from birdies that fly
And compose you a tune

Give you loving warm as mama's oven
And if that don't do . . .

Then I'll try something new

When I was through, I turned around and hugged Daddy so hard I nearly hurt him.

"Boy, what's wrong with you?"

113

"I think I just got myself a hit, Daddy."

"Well, give it to Cleveland. They need a hit worse than you."

"I need a hit, Smokey. Everyone around here has hits except us."

Diane Ross was still impatient, still anxious to see some chart action for the Supremes.

"When it happens," I told her, "it'll be like a bolt of lightning."

"Are you sure, Smokey?"

"I'm not sure of anything, baby, except that the sun's gonna set and the tax man's gonna call."

"What can I be doing that I'm not doing to push us forward?"

"You're pushing, honey. I've never seen anyone push so much. I'd say you're doing fine."

"But the hit, I've got to have a hit . . ."

Later that year, "I'll Try Something New," sung by the Miracles, hit big. The Supremes still hadn't made it, but our career was going great guns, and, better yet, Claudette became pregnant again. This time, we were sure, there'd be no mishap. This time we just had to make it . . .

Killing and Cooperating

By 1963 the pot was boiling. By 1964 it had boiled over. By 1965 we were scorching. And from then on things only got hotter.

It was wild; at times it seemed chaotic and chancy, but, believe me, there was a method to Berry's madness.

From the get-go, Motown was a hotbed of competition. Berry liked it that way, and so did I. That was our background, the streets where we grew up, battling and boxing and beating down contenders until we were crowned champs.

In those early days we'd have killer Ping-Pong tournaments, killer chess tournaments, killer poker games. Passive cats couldn't survive Motown. No one wanted to lose. Berry built himself a company of winners. That same feeling was infused in the music: writers and producers would kill for a smash—work 'round the clock, edit and reedit and edit some more. The artists moved with similar motivation, singing their asses off to get a hit.

Though competition flamed the fire in our hearts, we also glowed with warm love for each other. Somehow, these two emotions lived side by side. We were rivals and we were friends—Tops and Temps, Miracles and Marvelettes—we helped each other while trying to top each other.

Motown ran on creative juices. Most record companies were headed by cats who were primarily businessmen. But because Berry was a songwriter and producer, because his heart was more excited by music than balance sheets, his firm followed musical feelings. The song—the hit song— was an obsession that filled our nights and days. We dreamed it, we pursued it, we did it. In fact, for a period of time, we did it bigger than anybody—before or since.

We did it in this little building, this old house called Hitsville.

We loved that house, until we'd spend more time there than home. The house was part of the magic. The house was our hangout. It was also our studio and recreation center. It had to be the most energetic spot on the planet. Miss Lily would make us meals and we'd make ourselves sick from laughing so hard, from working so hard, making some friend- ships that would last a lifetime. Others, you'll see, would die a hard death.

There were warnings. When the money started coming in, Berry called us together and put it plainly:

"Look," he said, "y'all are getting some hefty checks now, but remember—the bread is not all yours. A big chunk be- longs to Uncle Sam. Eventually, Sam's gonna get his, so you better put his aside right now. If you don't do it now, you'll lose it later."

Of all the people in the room—writers, producers and artists—I may have been the only one who listened.

Berry was far from perfect. He made mistakes about sing- ers and songs; sometimes the pressure got to him; he could go off; he could be moody; and, later, he didn't always hire the right executives. But his goals were clear, his values solid. In the beginning, for instance, he sent his artists to school. Fact is, he created a school. Called it Artist Development and hired Harvey Fuqua to run the thing.

All the teachers were steeped in knowledge and strict as hell. Vocal coach Maurice King was an exacting taskmaster. The great choreographer Cholly Atkins turned us into dancers. Maxine Powell taught us fundamental social graces, giving us the confidence to walk into any situation with our heads high.

If comaraderie and competition were Hitsville characteristics, so was criticism. Berry Gordy is one of the most critical people in the world. He built Motown by criticizing—to the point of pain—every song and every production. He was unmerciful. If he could punch a hole in your product, he would. If he couldn't, he knew it was bulletproof and had a chance at chart action.

"We don't have the connections," he told me, "or the deep pockets. That's why we have to make it on talent and talent alone. If our quality falls, we'll fall with it."

Quality people were all around me.

Walking into the rehearsal hall, I ran into Lamont Dozier sitting at the piano, playing with a Bo Diddley–derived dance ditty.

"Hey, man," I said, "what's that?"

"Not sure."

He noodled some more, and the shit sounded even better.

"That a new song, Lamont?"

"Not sure."

I was sure liking it, though.

"Got any words?"

"Only these." He started humming, "Lum dee lum dee la."

"Let me try," I said, imitating his scat licks. "I like it, Lamont. Man, I like it a lot."

"Then you got it."

The Miracles cut it; Lamont and Brian Holland produced it; and "Mickey's Monkey" climbed to the top of the tree, creating a full-fledged dance craze while becoming our big hit of 1963.

In 1963, Pete's army stint was up. (I wasn't drafted because of respiratory problems and a mastoidectomy which, according to army doctors, had left a hole in my head, a drainage opening that never closed.) The Miracles were back at full strength. Claudette, however, worked less and less. She had successful surgery on both her feet, but was feeling so good we had no doubt her pregnancy would go full term.

"Boo Boo," I said to her, "I know we're going to make it this time."

I bought a crib, a changing table, blankets and dozens of little baby toys. Man, I was ready.

But it didn't happen.

Like the first time, her water broke in the fifth month. Our hearts broke so badly that for days we just sat in the house, holding hands, praying for peace of mind. Comfort came on the wings of prolonged pain. Comfort came in the form of the deepening love between Claudette and me. But there was still a hole in our hearts where the baby might have been. And we promised ourselves we'd keep trying. And we did.

Tears and Tracks

I told you before and I'll tell you again: Marv Tarplin is a monster musician. He's inspired me all my life, and, especially in these formative years, he kicked my ass, coming up with music just begging for words. On the frets on his guitar, he gave birth to a slew of smash songs. Subtlety was Marv's hallmark—the tasty riff, the slight suggestion, the soulful turn of phrase. With just a few notes, Marv could whip up an emotional hurricane.

The first track he gave me haunted me for months before I found words to fit the music. Slowly I fleshed out the verses. I was dealing with a sad story, a cat who'd been cut deep, hurt by heartache. I knew my man was suffering strong. What I lacked, though, was a chorus.

One day I was working with Pete Moore when the picture finally focused: I saw a guy who'd cried so much until it looked like tears had walked over his face. *The tracks of my tears,* I thought to myself. I had the song.

That happened on a Friday. I worked all weekend on a demo tape, and the following Monday morning I showed up, bright-eyed and bushy-tailed, for the weekly meeting with all the other writers and producers.

The session started at 9:00, but you better get your ass there by 8:45, 'cause once they closed those doors, they wouldn't open again even if the Lord Himself had a song to sell.

You'd look around this big table and see the Motown brain trust—General Gordy at the helm surrounded by his lieutenants, Harvey Fuqua, Johnny Bristol, Mickey Stevenson, Brian Holland, Lamont Dozier, Eddie Holland, Clarence Paul—Stevie's main man—and, a little later, the formidable Norman Whitfield.

None of these guys were pushovers.

"Who's got something for the Supremes?" Berry would ask.

He built the meeting around the artists; anyone with a song for the Supremes, for example, would play it. Then came the critiques. Sometimes we'd all agree on what seemed an obvious hit. But mostly revisions would be suggested, and mostly they'd be heeded.

When we got to the Miracles that morning, I proudly played my tape of "The Tracks of My Tears."

"You crazy?" Berry asked when I was through.

"No. Why?"

"You got a hit, but you buried your hook. Bring it up at the end, man. Repeat that shit—that 'it's easy to trace the tracks of my tears' refrain—until you wear it out."

The song wore well. It was a Miracles hit in the mid-sixties, a Linda Ronstadt hit in the mid-seventies, and, in the mid-eighties, a hit in the movie *Platoon*. The movie meant the most; it gave me special joy to know that, in some small way, our tune comforted guys risking their lives for a cause most of us still don't understand.

*   *   *

"I don't understand, Smoke," Marvin Gaye was saying. "I had one hit, but it wasn't what I expected. I still want to sing those standards."

It was the middle of March and we were playing catch on the lawn in front of the Hitsville building. Marvin threw a pretty pass. The wind was kicking up and the Andantes, one of our better female vocal groups, were gossiping on the porch. An occasional fan would pass by and wave, recognizing either Marvin or me.

"You tried the standards once, Dad, and it didn't work."

"But I got a plan, man," said Marvin, looking at me in his sly-eyed manner. "I got a different approach. Maybe if I sing a whole album of Nat Cole songs."

"Holland-Dozier-Holland's got some songs for your ass. And I got a few myself."

"The standards," Dad would say, "I'm gonna score with the standards."

He'd already scored with "Stubborn Kinda Fella," a self-describing number if there ever was one. He'd written it with George Gordy and Mickey Stevenson and used the Vandellas on backgrounds.

Mickey was director of A&R (Artists and Repertoire) and one of Motown's main characters. Martha Reeves was his secretary. She was also bonkers for Berry. Mickey was a musical cat who reminded me of Kingfish on *Amos and Andy*. Always wheeling and dealing. He'd run shit on you, then look up to see if you were buying his bull. "When the song comes out," he'd say, angling for a piece of the writer's share, "I'll straighten you out."

Angling was part of those early days. The company couldn't have survived without it. We've been accused, for example, of performing at deejay-sponsored shows in exchange for airplay. Damn right we did! It was not only the right move, it was a brilliant move. We didn't believe in paying under the table, and what other means did we have of being heard? The fight for airplay was brutal and, hell yes, we used every legal means at our disposal.

I loved the company, but sometimes I hated company business. Remember once coming back from a long tour of the South. It'd been an especially rough trip, one of those instances when the Miracles decided to participate in a sit-in.

We'd been in Mississippi and gone to a lunch counter. Just sat there and waited, looking at one of those "we reserve the right to refuse service" signs hanging over our heads. We knew they wanted our black asses out of there. But that's just why we stayed, stayed over an hour until this redneck waiter saw we weren't leaving and asked what we wanted. Ordered a sandwich and a Coke, and don't you know it took another hour before the food arrived. Cat practically threw the shit at me, and I almost threw it back. I wanted to level him, wanted to fry him on his greasy grill, but my teacher was Martin Luther King and his teachers were Mahatma Gandhi and Jesus Christ. I had great examples to follow.

Following the southern route was hell. Most hotels were hostile to blacks, so you'd be stuck in funky boardinghouses on the wrong side of the tracks. You had to watch what you said, how you looked and where you walked. I hated the whole thing, and by the time I got back to Detroit, after driving all day and night, the last thing I wanted was to be woken up on a Tuesday morning with Berry Gordy talkin' 'bout me coming to some jive-ass 10:00 a.m. meeting.

"Can't make it," I told him on the phone. "Just got off the road, man. I'm beat. Need to go back to sleep."

"I need you there, Smoke."

"Damnit, Berry, this ain't right. I haven't slept in forty-eight hours. I'm dead."

"Be there at ten."

Berry can be cold, I thought to myself, dragging my ass out of bed, splashing water on my face and getting dressed.

I arrived a little late. Berry was in his office, surrounded by the company's top executives.

"I expect my people to be right on time," Berry scolded me.

Damn, I kept thinking, *this dude is a first-class asshole.*

"I especially like my vice presidents to be on time," he said, looking me dead in the eye.

Still groggy, I was confused. But when the other guys started applauding me, and Berry was all smiles, I saw the light: I was a Motown vice president, and suddenly I didn't feel tired or cranky anymore.

"I'm beginning to feel a little cranky, Smoke."

It was Aretha on the long-distance wire. She'd signed a contract with Columbia and was living in New York.

"What's the problem, baby?"

"I don't know. It seems like they won't really let me be me."

"What do you mean?"

"The records I'm putting out are turntable hits, but they're not really selling. I've got so much music stored up inside me, Smoke, I can hardly stand it."

"The record business is funny, Ree, but, believe me, with all your talent they can't keep you down for long."

Busting Through

My responsibility was new talent, which is why I can testify that much of what's been written about Motown's manipulations is unadulterated bullshit. I signed the acts; I saw the contracts; I know that the deals offered were straight-ahead and, for those days, standard as the twelve-bar blues.

The writers received their royalties like clockwork. Motown, through Jobete Music, published the songs and owned the copyrights, but why not? That was industry policy; record companies exploited the songs written by their artists and staff writers. When that policy started changing in the early seventies, Motown started changing as well. In fact, you'll see that some of the Motown artists—like Marvin Gaye and Stevie Wonder—set a pace for the industry to follow.

"Smoke, have you been following my new record?" Diane asked me. "It's burnin' up the charts."

We were walking up West Grand Boulevard to Cunningham's drug store down the street from Hitsville. Diane was bubbling over.

Inside, she ordered a banana split and I got me a double chocolate milkshake.

"You realize, Smokey," she continued, "that 'Where Did Our Love Go' is number-one pop?"

"Being on that Dick Clark tour, y'all got all kinds of exposure. I'm really happy for you, baby."

"This is just the beginning," she said, scooping off the whipped cream. "I can just feel it."

By 1964, the Supremes' and Four Tops' long list of Holland-Dozier-Holland mega-hits had begun. Berry poured a large part of the profits back into the company. He bought four other two-story houses on West Grand. He also bought himself a mansion in my childhood neighborhood, on Boston Boulevard, just down the street from where Cecil and Aretha lived with their dad, Reverend C. L. Franklin.

Where there used to be old beat-up Fords and Chevys parked in front of the Motown bungalows, now you'd see Cadillacs in every color of the rainbow. Soon as the new models came out, we'd be down at the dealers, scooping them up. Diamonds would be flashing, furs flying, gold glittering.

It was great while it lasted, but in show business, like life, nothing's certain, and as soon as some of those folks stopped making money or found the tax man breaking down their doors, they didn't blame themselves—God forbid!—they blamed Berry. Long as they were having hits and generating cash, Berry was God. But the minute the hits stopped or their money got funny, Berry was Satan.

Berry was in a peculiar spot. He liked hanging out at Hitsville with the cats—shooting pool, playing poker—but he also had to be the boss. "If I'm not a hard-ass," he once told me after firing a friend, "this place will go belly-up, and I'll have no one to blame but myself."

When the Supremes started their string of smashes—"Where Did Our Love Go?" "Baby Love," "Come See About Me," "Stop! In the Name of Love," "Back in My Arms Again"—Berry decided to manage the group himself. He saw their potential for even greater profit. He knew he needed to protect his property—after all, we'd discovered and developed the Supremes—against the wolves in the industry. And, by booking them on national TV shows and high-paying supper clubs, he opened the doors for the rest of us, expanding our market from the chitlin circuit to the concert halls of Paris, London and Rome.

I myself was looking to expand. I especially liked cashing those thousand-dollar bonus checks we'd get for writing number-one hits. As a producer I was always looking for the sleeping giants at Motown, the singers being overlooked. Fortunately, I found two.

The first was David Ruffin of the Temptations. I loved that group. I knew them back before they were the Primes, when they were the Distants. I liked the way the cats looked, each of them tall, thin and handsome. I called them the Five Deacons and grooved on their inventive background blends.

I had a happy history with the Temps.

The first thing I'd done on them—"I Want a Love I Can See"—sold locally, but they were still looking for their first national hit. I thought I found it when, driving into Detroit, Bobby Rogers helped me finish "The Way You Do the Things You Do."

When we got home I told Berry about the song.

"Don't bother, Smoke," Berry told me. "I already got a hit tune for the Temps."

"But, Berry," I insisted, "I got the sure-enough smash."

"We're about to release mine."

"Will you give me a couple of days to record my thing?"

"Go ahead, but I'm telling you, Smoke, you're wasting your time."

Couple of days later, even after hearing "The Way You Do the Things You Do," Berry still wasn't convinced.

"Like mine better," he said.

"Let's test them."

"Why?" he asked.

"Afraid of losing?" I wanted to know.

"Hell, no. Let's go."

We played it for secretaries, for the postman, for people passing by on the street; we played it for anyone we could find. And I'm proud to report that Berry Gordy, genius that he is, didn't get a single vote.

We released "The Way You Do the Things You Do," with Eddie Kendricks singing lead, and the Temps had their big record.

Now I dug Eddie, but I saw David back there, waiting to explode.

Finally, with the help of Ronnie White, I wrote something I knew was right for Ruffin. It happened when the Miracles and Temps were on the same week-long bill at the Apollo. In between shows, I'd drag David down to the piano, where I'd show him this song while the other Temps honed their harmonies.

Back in Detroit, we cut the sucker. So many things were happening so quickly, I soon forgot about it.

Couple of months later, Berry called me to the office.

"Man, I got some serious news for you."

"Good or bad?"

"The best."

"A check?"

"For a cool thousand."

"Fantastic!" My first thought was that the Miracles' "Ooo Baby Baby" had gone number one.

"It's not the Miracles, it's the Temps."

"The tune I cut on David?"

"Last year 'My Guy' went number one on Mary Wells," said Berry, grinning ear to ear, "but this year this new one, this 'My Girl,' is gonna be even bigger. David Ruffin's gonna be a star, and your song's gonna be a legend."

Some folks figured I wrote "Don't Mess with Bill" about myself. Wrong. Just liked the way the name sung. It was a song I wrote and produced on the Marvelettes. Up till then, Gladys Horton had handled the leads. But Wanda Young had caught my ear with her sexy country voice. I saw her as untapped talent. So I tailor-made the tune for her, and was thrilled when it sold like gangbusters.

Nothing thrilled me more, though, than helping out Dad.

Marvin Gaye was hurting. Sales-wise, he was in a valley. His Sinatra plan had fizzled and, like everyone else at Motown, he was hungry for a hit. Marv Tarplin had whipped up an especially nasty riff, a hot hook that took off the top of my head. *I'll be doggone!* I thought to myself, mesmerized by Marv's music.

Went in and cut the song on Dad who sang the shit out

129

of it. I loved producing Marvin Gaye. He'd interpret my material like he'd written it himself, improvising and improving the original concept. Dad was brilliant.

"I'll Be Doggone" was a top-five worldwide hit, and so was the follow-up we wrote for Dad, born out of another killer Marv Tarplin riff, "Ain't That Peculiar."

It's also peculiar that in this same time frame we were accused of hiding our blackness. The Miracles' *Mickey's Monkey* album, for instance, features a cartoon on the cover instead of a photo of the group. We'd also signed the Isley Brothers—in fact, my "Way Over There" had been inspired by the driving beat of their "Shout"—and their first Motown album, *This Old Heart of Mine*, showed two white lovers on a beach. Some critics said we were trying to fool folks into thinking the artists were white.

Those art-cover concepts, though, didn't have shit to do with covering up our color. Hell, by then everyone knew that the Miracles and Isleys were black. There was nothing to hide. We were just looking for devices to attract attention. And those devices did; the albums sold.

Despite all this success, though, 1964 left a bitter taste in my mouth: my woman had another miscarriage. We were especially despondent because the doctor felt that if Claudette stayed off the road, her chances would increase. We listened to him, but lost the fetus all the same.

"Maybe we're trying too hard, baby," I said to her, trying to heal the hurt. "Maybe we should cool it for a while. Why don't you rejoin the group when we go to Europe? I'd hate to see Europe without you."

"I'm not sure what I want to do. I just know that I don't want to disappoint you, Doo."

"You've never done that, baby, and you never will."

Claudette came to Europe with us. It was her last tour with the Miracles, though she continued to record with us until I myself quit in 1972.

When we got home we settled into a house—our first ever—at 19357 Santa Barbara. It was modest, but to us it was beautiful. We liked the neighborhood—Marvin and Anna lived right around the corner on Outer Drive—and there was a big basement downstairs where I put a pool table. There were four bedrooms, plenty of room to fill the house with kids.

"It'll happen," I promised Claudette.

We hadn't given up hope; we were just afraid of being hurt again.

Golf Don't Care
about You

If you're not looking, golf will hook you and keep you hooked. Happened to me in the late sixties. Nearly twenty years later, I'm still a goner. Golf has no mercy.

Golf called to me in the form of his disciples, Ronnie White, Harvey Fuqua, Robert Gordy, Mickey Stevenson and Johnny Bristol. The boys took me out to Detroit's Palmer Park course and showed me the ropes. Told me I was doing great; told me I had talent; said, "swing this way," "swing that way," "put your foot here," "put your foot there." The cats taught me soul golf. Fact is, they taught me wrong. It was all good natured, but they sure didn't mind making bets and taking my money.

Now golf don't care how you get bit, just as long as you do get bit. And back then, we were *all* bitten, Berry included.

We'd get to the office early, write, record, do our business, and by noon be out at the links. Berry would even take us on golf trips to Las Vegas and the Bahamas, where he'd rent houses for us, turning them into all-male dorms.

Marvin Gaye started playing, too, but he'd get hoodwinked by the hustlers. Those guys would be waiting for him, like wolves waiting for the sheep. Dad always had a plan to beat them, but never did. Me, I was being bested by my friends until another friend named Forest Hairston set me straight.

I was out there one spring day, soaking up the sun and lining up the ball to slice it. Everyone had me down for every bet, but just before I swung, Forest stepped in my way.

"Motherfucker," he said, knocking my ball off the tee, "you are *not* gonna hit that ball like that again. Only way you gonna hit that ball like that is to hit it through me. You come out here every day while these dudes skin you alive. I know they're your friends and they love you, but they love your money too. They ain't giving you no righteous advice, which is what you need."

Suddenly a hush fell over the land, like in the E. F. Hutton commercials.

"First of all," Forest continued, "line your ass up straight, square up to the ball and hit it."

I hit it like he said, and the thing went straight down the fairway.

"Now," he suggested, "meet me at the practice tee and I'll straighten your shit out."

He did. I practiced, I worked hard, I hedged my bets and honed my skills. I got better. I began winning. Forest, I love you.

But golf will fool you. Golf will let you get good for a minute, and then, a minute later, frustrate you to tears. Golf has no favorites; golf shows no mercy.

Golf will get you going—like it got me going in the sixties —and hold you in its spell for the rest of your life. Golf is the addiction no one beats. It's the heroin of sports. Golf is deep.

Changing Venues

There was a time when for a buck-fifty you could go to the Fox Theater in Detroit and see the Marvelettes, Mary Wells, Martha and the Vandellas, the Supremes, Little Stevie Wonder, the Tops, Temps, Miracles and Marvin Gaye, all kicked off by Junior Walker and the All-Stars.

Junior was such a tremendous trooper—a big-sound stomp-down saxist—that once at the Fox he was dancing so hard, he tripped and fell into the orchestra pit. The pit was deep, but Junior was a showman, and he kept playing—his wail growing more distant the farther he fell—until he landed on his feet, his "Shotgun" still firing. The man never missed a note.

I'm glad that Claudette didn't miss Europe. We found our fans there as fanatical as the dolls and dudes in Detroit. It was wonderful to learn that we were loved by people living so far away.

Met the Beatles at a private club called the White Elephant. They'd already recorded "You Really Got a Hold On Me," a song I wrote inspired by Sam Cooke's "Bring It On Home to Me." They were not only respectful of us, they were down-right worshipful. Whenever reporters asked them about their influences, they'd go into euphoria about Motown. I dug them, not only for their songwriting talent, but their honesty.

I was honestly excited by every country we visited. For the first time I saw that our music, born in a working-class neighborhood of a certain city in a certain country, tran-scended all boundaries and borders. Our lyrics and melodies were touching young hearts all over the world.

Back in America, Motown owned the charts. Our batting average—hits per releases—was the highest in history. And it was a particular kick in the ass to know that the artists doing it were friends.

Take the Tops. I mentioned that growing up, no one would challenge the Four Aims—Levi Stubbs, Obie Benson, Duke Fakir and Lawrence Payton. When they joined Motown the Aims turned into Tops, and their singing turned on the multitudes. If, like paintings, they hung voices in museums, Levi's would be hanging in the Louvre next to the *Mona Lisa.* His big beautiful sound—listen to him belt out "Baby, I Need Your Loving" or "Bernadette"—is a priceless work of art. And Lawrence, let it be known, was the cat who taught us singers modern jazz harmony. He had all those Hi-Lo/Four Freshmen voicings down pat. Just for the love of it, Lawrence patiently showed the other Motown vocalists the slickest, hippest background blends.

People started talking about a Motown sound.

What was it?

Swooping string arrangements by Paul Riser; infectiously gritty grooves ground out by one of the funkiest rhythm sections in human history—pianist Earl Van Dyke, bassist James Jamerson, drummer Benny Benjamin, guitarists Robert

White, Eddie Willis and Joe Messina; killer charts by cats like Hank Cosby and Gil Askey; the striking sound of singers like Diane and David and Mary and Martha. It was a mixture of all this—and more.

The Motown sound was a miracle. It spoke for—it was born from—a special time and place: Detroit, Michigan, in the sixties. It was the combination of an astonishing range of talents, politics and personalities, people who were naive, happy, hungry for money, looking to be loved and accepted, dying to compete, burning with ambition, blazing with talent—first raw, then refined and finally irresistible. It was black music too damn good—too accessible, too danceable, too romantic, too real—not to be loved by everyone.

Then why was I miserable playing the Copacabana?

Picture it:

New York City. The high rollers out in force, the average age of the Copa patron forty-five, maybe fifty. Cats in tuxes, chicks in minks, everyone expecting to hear "Moon River" or "Melancholy Baby." Back then, rock 'n' roll hadn't hit the nightclub crowd.

The Supremes did great at these gigs—their act was glitzy—but we were new at it; we were nervous. Psychologically and vocally, I wasn't ready. I was forced to sing songs I considered cornball, material that fell outside my character. I've never liked going places where I couldn't be me; never liked singing tunes where I couldn't express me; and at the Copa, I felt far removed from myself.

Worse, the joint was a workhouse—three grueling shows a night. The stage was nonexistent, you were practically dancing on the customers' plates, and reputedly the management was Mafia. Not too pleasant, except for one night when the place served a purpose.

One of the Miracles had been seeing a wild woman. For mental health's sake, he decided to end the relationship, but this chick wouldn't have it. She refused the rejection, screaming and scratching and finally, when that wouldn't do, threatening to have his ass killed.

"You'll never get through your act alive," she promised. "I'm having someone shoot you through the throat, *tonight.*"

Not exactly comforting words uttered four hours before the show.

Our road manager wanted to inform the cops, but the Copa management said that they could handle the situation. Could they ever!

When we arrived, from the limo to the dressing room there was a double line of dudes who looked like the kind of Mafia soldiers you see in the movies. Inside the club, ringed around the wall, another squadron of stern-looking cats stood menacingly in dark pin-striped suits and red silk ties. Not a hint of trouble all night. Never felt so protected in my life.

Never felt more bugged at Berry than when we did *Ed Sullivan* for the first time.

Berry can be nervous. And when Berry's nervous, you're nervous. Doing our debut national TV show, he was more nervous than us. We had our act together; we'd planned a medley of our own hits plus a version of "Yesterday" for which Maurice King wrote a beautiful vocal arrangement and Marv Tarplin accompanied us on his fluttering guitar.

"Sure you know your routine, Smoke?" Berry asked for the tenth time.

"Sure I'm sure."

"Get the guys," he demanded, "so we can go back to your room and rehearse some more."

"Don't need more rehearsing."

"I say you do."

So we did. Berry critiqued, cautioned and cajoled us, stressing and restressing the importance of this appearance.

"This could be the difference between life and death," he declared.

"This could be the end of our friendship," I joked under my breath. But I knew better; I knew Berry just wanted us to be our best.

Finally, mercifully, the moment of truth arrived.

Ed Sullivan—a mystery man if there ever was one—came to the mike while we waited in the wings. "Ladies and gentlemen," he said, "let's have a warm welcome for a great group of guys from Detroit, Michigan—Smokey and the Little Smokeys!"

No matter, we went out there and tore it up.

"It's tearing me up, man."

I was backstage with Marvin Gaye at the Coconut Grove in L.A.

"What's bothering you, Dad?"

"I've got this problem, Smoke. I can just look at the pussy and come."

The way Marvin said it, both of us couldn't help but laugh.

"Well, man, why do you think that happens to you?" I asked.

"Women expect so much of me, Smoke, they've made me into this sex symbol thing until sometimes it just messes with my head."

This is really messing with my head, I said to myself as Marvin was onstage rocking the crowd with "How Sweet It Is." *That cat over there has my family's face, yet I can't place the dude.*

Finally, after the show, I went over and asked him.

"Hey, man, don't I know you?"

"I don't know, but I know who you are."

"Well, where you from?"

"I'm really from Detroit, but now I'm the program director for KGFJ in Los Angeles."

"What's your name?"

"I'm Roland Bynum."

"Bynum! What's your mother's name, man?"

"I don't know, I was raised by foster parents."

Suddenly I grabbed him and hugged him.

"You're my nephew!" I shouted. "Your mother's my sister!"

Now he hugged me back and we started crying tears of joy. I began to explain, "Bynum's my big sister's maiden name. You're her second son, born between my nephew Tyrone and my niece Sharon. Big Sister was so poor then, she had to give you up for adoption. But you're my nephew, man, you really are."

Must have stayed up all night, hugging and crying and laughing and thinking of how weird it was that he'd played my records and I'd heard him on the radio without either of us knowing we were family.

Back home, thoughts of a family were still haunting me and Claudette. With each pregnancy our hope was renewed. We tried to view each conception as though it were the first, a springtime filled with fertile promise and fresh love.

When Claudette became pregnant for the fifth time—or maybe the sixth, we started losing count—we both did a great deal of praying.

"This time," said Claudette, always brave, always optimistic, "I feel different, I feel stronger."

This time, I thought silently, *our prayers will be answered.*

PART THREE

Agonies and Ecstasies

Mirage

"Sweetness," I once wrote in a song, "is only heartache's camouflage. The love I saw in you is just a mirage."

Maybe I was starting to doubt, maybe I saw any child born to me and Claudette as a mirage, maybe I was afraid of watching my wife suffer more pain. Either way, I fought my fears and tried to stay positive.

The first few months were rough. Each time Claudette moaned or groaned, I got scared. Each time I took her to the doctor, I was afraid of bad news.

The doctor, though, gave us good reports. "Nothing to worry about," he said.

By the fourth month I saw that Claudette's skin was glowing and her eyes sparkling. By the fifth month she was absolutely radiant. And by the middle of the sixth month, when I left to perform at Palisades Park in New Jersey, I was feeling really confident about Claudette.

I was also feeling good about my career. Tunes I'd written for the Miracles—"Going to a Go Go" and "Choosey Beggar"—were selling. So were my songs on the Temps—"It's Growing," "Since I Lost My Baby" and "Get Ready." Also had two more big records on the Marvelettes, a funky thing called "The Hunter Gets Captured by the Game" and "My Baby Must Be a Magician." Creatively, I was flowing.

It was a magical night, performing under a warm star-filled sky, fans dancing, girls grabbing at us, guys calling out for our hits.

At the end of the show, I went to our dressing room and had started changing when my niece Sylvia knocked on the door.

"Call home, Smoke," she said. "Claudette just gave birth to twin girls."

"What! Are they all right?"

"They're tiny, it's touch and go, but the doctor is hoping they can make it."

Make it, make it, dear God, let the babies make it, I prayed, getting no news over the phone, racing to the airport, boarding the plane, flying to Detroit. *Twins are a double blessing, twins would more than make up for all the past pain, twins are everything we could hope for . . .*

"The twins are dead," said the doctor when I breathlessly arrived at the hospital. "Their respiratory systems have collapsed."

He might as well have run a stake through my heart. I felt myself boiling with rage. I wanted to kill the doctor, kill the nurses, kill anyone who'd been unable to save our babies. Besides, why hadn't the doctor heard two heartbeats during Claudette's last exam? Why didn't he know she was having twins?

Instead of asking these questions, I went to the morgue. I wanted to see the infants; I wanted to know their faces.

Lying perfectly still, they appeared as miniature angels. One girl looked like me, the other had Claudette's beautiful features. Their arms, their cheeks, their hands, their fingers, even their tiny fingernails . . . everything was so delicately, so perfectly formed. It was as though any second now their eyelids would flutter open. They'd look at me, their father, and I'd hear them breathe, I'd see them smile.

Finally, though, they were no more than a mirage.

Back in her hospital room, Claudette couldn't be comforted.

"I let you down again, Doo," she said through tears.

"That's crazy, Boo Boo." Gently, I kissed her eyes. "You didn't let anyone down."

"It keeps happening, I keep failing."

"You gotta get those notions out of your head, Claudette. I didn't know those babies, but I know you, and I'm just glad you're all right. I feel blessed that you're my wife. We love each other, and that's all that matters."

"I still feel like it's my fault."

I tried to console her, but it wasn't working. After hours of sitting by her side, I left the hospital and went home. I couldn't sleep, though. Kept thinking of how Claudette was blaming herself, how she was worrying that my love for her had lessened.

I went to the piano and started writing:

This is no fiction, this is no act
This is real; it's a fact
I'll always belong only to you
Each day I'll be living to
Make sure I'm giving you
More love, and more joy
Than either age or time could ever destroy
My love will be so sound
It'll take about a hundred lifetimes to live it down

"More Love" was the song. That same sad year, it was a hit for the Miracles.

People have asked me about my inspiration for writing songs, and I've answered that sometimes stories come from real life and sometimes I just make them up. This was real life.

Singing "More Love," I could think only of Claudette, hoping my words would help heal her heart.

Christmas came. We tried to be jolly, but it wasn't easy. It was a blustery winter, snow squalls nearly every day, temperatures below zero. I braved the storms, fought my blues and went shopping with a friend and fellow Motown writer Al Cleveland.

"Need to buy something really nice for Claudette," I said. "Let's go to Hudson's."

Hudson's was hip, the biggest and best department store in downtown Detroit. The holiday hustle and bustle—merry decorations, folks piled up with packages—got me to feeling a little better. I avoided the toys and baby department, heading straight for the jewelry counter.

Picked out some pearls for Claudette. "They're beautiful," I told the saleslady. "Just hope my wife likes them."

"I second that emotion," said Al.

What a funny phrase, I kept thinking on the way home, dodging in and out of holiday traffic.

That afternoon we wrote the song. "I Second That Emotion" was soon a smash for the Miracles.

That night, at the annual Motown Christmas party in the Hitsville building, my spirit was happier. Writing had released some of the sadness inside me.

Everyone was there, drinking, dancing, playing poker, poking fun. In those days the Spinners were with us—it bugged me that we could never get a hit on them, they were sensational singers—and so were Gladys Knight and her Pips.

From across the room, I heard someone call my name.

It was Stevie Wonder. Whether it's your vibe or your scent, Stevie will sniff you out in a minute.

He came over to greet me. "Merry Christmas, Stevie," I said. "How are you?"

Now I know he's blind, but he thinks I'm deaf 'cause of how he puts his mouth right up against my ear when he talks to me.

"I need your help, Smoke. Hank Cosby and I wrote this music, but we can't think of any words. Will you write the lyrics?"

"I'll try."

Then, as he often does, Stevie started rapping, going on forever in the most abstract terms. I tried sneaking away, but he followed, never letting me out of his sight.

A little later, inspired by his track, I wrote "The Tears of a Clown." We put it out on a Miracles album and nothing happened. Years would pass before I heard from the song again, and when I did, it would play heavily on my life.

"My life is changing, Smoke," said Marvin Gaye. "I'm going out for the Detroit Lions football team."

"You're going out of your mind."

"I'm in my sweats and I'm on my way over to your place. Get ready. We're going running!"

Ten minutes later Dad was at my front door, huffing and puffing. I was nuts enough to follow suit. We made our way in the snow and slush, running for miles. When we finally got back home, Marvin led us through a half hour of jumping jacks and push-ups, all in the freezing cold.

"Those monsters will murder you, Marvin."

"I got a plan, man."

"You got a problem, Dad. You're insane."

"I just want to catch a kick-off at Tiger Stadium and run it back for a touchdown, just once."

Dad actually showed up at training camp, where he actually got his ass kicked. I knew players from other teams who told me, "Tell Marvin to keep singing. We love his music, but if he shows up on the field, we'll send him home in a box."

"I'm going to be a boxer," was Dad's next declaration. He'd have me down at the gym watching him spar. He said he was serious about professional fighting.

"I'm serious about how you're always falling into bullshit, Dad. Why don't you just stick to singing?"

A few months later he stuck it to us all singing "Heard It Through the Grapevine." Here's what happened:

Norman Whitfield had been turning the Motown sound around. Influenced by Sly Stone, he produced psychedelic-sounding stuff on the Temps like "Cloud Nine." With Barrett Strong, he'd also written "Grapevine" and cut it on the Miracles. But nothing happened on the song until Aretha and Otis Redding got into a little friendly rivalry.

"Hey, Ree," Otis said one day when the three of us happened to hook up backstage at the Regal Theater in Chicago. "I recorded that song you did, 'Try A Little Tenderness.' The only difference is, my version's a hit," he laughed.

"That's okay, sucker," said Aretha. "I'm about to throw down on one of your tunes. When I'm through with it, you won't even recognize the thing."

Leaving for London in 1964.

Claudette and Sidney Poitier at Freeport in the Bahamas in the mid-sixties.

Battling with Berry during a chess game in London, 1964.

Stepping at the Twenty Grand, Detroit. *Left*: bassist James Jamerson. *Right*: guitarist Marv Tarplin.

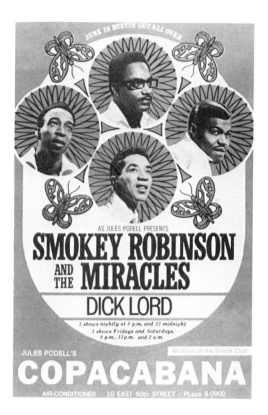

Unhappy venue.

Smokey and Claudette in Hollywood.

Marvin Tarplin.

I liked dressing for those cold
Detroit winters.

In the tub with Berry
in 1968.

Miss Lily, Mama Three.

Big Sister Gerry and Daddy Five.

Smokey and Five flying to Europe.

Tamla and Berry.

Mother's Day: Sisters Gerry and Rose Ella with
Claudette.

Claudette, *right*, with her best friend, Earlyn,
who died tragically of cancer in 1983.

The Miracles in the seventies.

Pops Gordy, one of my heroes.

Father and son.

Father and son.

The family, in our Beverly Hills backyard.

"Golf don't care about you." On the links in the seventies. *From left*: Harvey Fuqua, Smokey, Billy Eckstine and Ronnie White.

Smokey with Aretha
on *Soul Train*.

Smokey and manager Mike Roshkind.

My virtuoso vocalists: Ivory Stone, *left*, and
Pat Henley.

Berry and Smokey.

Daddy Five at eighty-three.

Trey.

Brother, brother. Leon Kennedy and Smokey.

The current band. *Standing, from left*: Larry Ball, Robert Bowles, Sonny Burke, David Ii, Tony Lewis, Chris Ho and Marv Tarplin. *Seated, from left*: Pat Henley, Smokey and Ivory Stone.

From left: Luther Vandross, Smokey, Dionne Warwick and Stevie Wonder.

Couple of months later, Aretha came out with "Respect," a thing of beauty and joy forever, a milestone in the annals of funk. By then, she'd switched to Atlantic where they allowed her to do her own thing. Finally, she got her due. She was an international star.

It was Ree's "Respect" that motivated Norman to recut "Grapevine" on Gladys Knight, using a similarly sassy soul feel. The result was a huge hit. But Whitfield wasn't through. He kept hearing his song differently. He wrote a haunting string chart and gave it to Dad who promptly sang the living shit out of it. Next thing we knew Marvin Gaye had the biggest single in Motown history. Man, how I loved sitting back and listening to that record!

Funny thing about Norman. While most of the producers liked the artists to interpret, Whitfield wouldn't stand for it. Had to have his songs sung just the way he wrote them. You might argue, but you might not; Norman had so many hits —that long string on the Temps ("Wish It Would Rain," "Runaway Child, Running Wild," "Psychedelic Shack," "Ball of Confusion," "Just My Imagination"), not to mention Edwin Starr's "War"—you might conclude that he knew what he was doing.

He did. And so did Ashford and Simpson.

Nick and Val did a gorgeous thing on us called "You Ain't Livin' Till You're Lovin'," but their greatest moments were with Dad and Tammi Terrell, and, a little later, Diana. "Ain't No Mountain High Enough" was another one of those songs strong enough to hit on two distinct occasions.

This was the time—the rise of Whitfield, the ascendancy of Ashford and Simpson—when Holland-Dozier-Holland fell out with Berry.

They each had made millions, but finally felt they'd make

more elsewhere. They sued us, never won anything and, to my mind, lost a great deal.

I blame Eddie Holland. I always saw Brian Holland and Lamont Dozier as the talents on that team. Eddie could write lyrics, but he'd often have others help him, forgetting to give them credit. I didn't like that. I thought his negativism got in brother Brian's way. And Lamont got T-rolled; he got caught in the middle.

Tried to talk Brian into staying.

"Man," I said, "I think you're going to find an awfully cold world waiting for you out there."

"You may be right, Smoke, but it's something we've got to do. And after all, Eddie is my brother."

They left and tried to build an empire of their own. They had a few hits for a couple of years, but after that, the rest has been silence.

I'll always love Brian and Lamont, because they helped make Motown, because they're beautiful writers and beautiful people, and because their music is immortal.

Things were changing. The business was rewarding us, but also hardening us. Even as Motown's main acts grew more popular, that initial period of euphoria was coming to a screeching stop. We started reexamining our lives and realized that, at least in many cases, we were hurting deep inside.

Broken Promises

When you're young, the world seems promising; there's the promise of friendship, success, a happy family, an exciting career. Motown gave promise to many. There'd been many Motown marriages—our Bobby Rogers married Wanda Young of the Marvelettes, Billy Gordon of the Contours married Georgeanna Dobbins, also of the Marvelettes; Johnny Bristol married Iris Gordy, Berry's niece; Mickey Stevenson married Kim Weston. In spirit and mind, Motown represented hope to a slew of young artists—a bunch of kids, really—looking to get over. Many of us did. Some of us didn't.

In an atmosphere where hit records were exploding like fireworks—over here, over there, everywhere you looked—it was easy to lose perspective. Grim reality raised its ugly head for the first time, I suppose, when our driver, Little Eddie, was killed down south. A couple of years later, Loucye Gordy, Berry's beloved sister who watched over our books, was struck down by a cerebral hemorrhage. Berry never forgave himself, always questioning his choice of doctors. In the midst of our greatest period of success, he suffered one of his greatest losses.

He'd also been married and separated from his third wife Margaret—from then on, Berry's bachelorhood was unshakable—this during a time when the Supremes had become the hottest act in the world. It's also the time that Florence Ballard, one of the original Supremes, fell away.

Florence was beautiful, big-voiced, fun-loving and down to earth. Her boyfriend, Tommy Chapman, had been Berry's driver. Little by little, he convinced Flo that Berry was out to get her. He messed with her mind. I think he pushed her off track, persuading her that there was more money to be made outside Motown. Florence also suffered from envy. She deluded herself by believing that she deserved the same recognition as Diana. She really believed she was as great a talent. Compounding the problem was Flo's own depression. She started drinking, showing up late, even missing gigs. It hurt to see it, but Florence did herself in. By 1968 she was out of the group; by 1976 she'd died of a heart attack.

Self-destruction took a similar toll on Paul Williams, one of the Temps, a friend I loved dearly. Riddled by personal problems and alcoholism, he shot himself to death in 1973.

Sometimes I think success is harder to accept than failure. The options open to you—drugs, drink, sex excess, ego-tripping—can wipe you out quicker than rejection. And then there's jealousy.

Books have been written about Diana Ross and Berry Gordy, their love affair, his favoritism, her bitchiness, his unfair treatment of the other Motown women.

Well, I was there; I saw it come down; and I'm here to report that, although they surely fell in love, theirs was a relationship rooted in business.

Berry managed Diana because Diana was a tremendous talent.

Diana followed Berry because Berry was a tremendous businessman. These were two powerful but practical people, interested, more than anything, in success.

At one time or another most of the Motown women—Florence, Mary Wilson, Martha Reeves, Gladys Knight—have complained about the attention lavished on Diana. What they don't say, though, and what's most evident, is that Diana's remarkable abilities as an entertainer kicked her up into another category. She demanded that attention; she earned it. She had the charisma to fill football stadiums full of fans all over the world; her TV specials were spectacular; in her first acting role, she won an Academy Award nomination.

I take nothing away from the others—great, soulful singers all. But Diana was different; her gift was overwhelming. She broke down barriers for the rest of us. Berry probably spoiled her, and, sure, she could be difficult, but what female superstar isn't? A woman not willing to wield a sharp sword will never cut through the bullshit of this business.

Diana's growth as an artist—first in the Supremes, then on her own—inspired me. I was proud of her. To me, she was a kid from my neighborhood, a part of my childhood, a buddy who had succeeded beyond anyone's wildest expectations.

Marvin Gaye's expectations of himself still weren't fulfilled.

We went to see him at Bimbo's, an elegant San Francisco supper club, where he came out in a top hat and cane, crooned "Me and My Shadow," and followed with a slew of standards. Finally, almost as an afterthought, he sang his hits—the songs the audience had come to hear—cramming them all into an abbreviated medley.

His fans were disappointed and, back in his dressing room, so was he.

"I'm going off to do something entirely different," said Dad in that whisper-quiet cagey cool voice of his.

"What?" I wanted to know.

"Can't say right now. But I'm forming a plan."

In the late sixties my own plans were changing. For the first time in my life, I was growing sick of show business. The traveling was getting to me. The politics were getting to me. The Vietnam war was raging; King and Kennedy were gunned down in cold blood. You'd have to be a robot not to feel despair in the air.

And, to top it off, I suffered one of the greatest losses of my entire life: my nephew Tyrone, as close to me as a twin brother, grew despondent over his inability to hold a job. Said he was tired of the whole thing, and killed himself. His death nearly killed me.

For the first time, I wanted to take time off from my career.

Then something personal happened—it took place in an airport—the aftershocks from which would quake for twenty years.

Angels and Witches

Her father came up to me. I remember the day like it was yesterday. We'd just arrived in Detroit. I was wearing a white Nehru suit and a gold chain, all the rage back then.

"My daughter is a fan of yours," he said. "She'd very much like to meet you."

"Of course," I agreed.

His daughter looked like she'd just stepped out of *Vogue*. Her name was Kandi and she was, in fact, a fashion model. She had flashing eyes, caramel-colored skin, a bright smile, a supershapely figure, a beautiful personality.

Was I vulnerable? Sometimes I think I'm always vulnerable to women. Sometimes I think most men are. In any event, on that afternoon, talking to her at the airport, nearly losing myself in her warmth, I nonetheless resisted.

"Nice to have met you," I said.

"You can't escape my spell," she joked. "I'm a witch."

"But I'm an angel," I replied. "And angels can escape witches whenever they want."

I escaped.

Until . . .

Some time later. We were playing the Michigan State Fair and, lurking in the wings, there she was, a vision of loveliness in high heels and tight dress, her attributes evident, her attitude open and friendly.

"I'm working as a model at the auto show," she said. "But my full-time job is at the Playboy Club. I'm a bunny."

I hopped down—never had been in a Playboy Club before—and watched her work. She gave me her number, and the first time I went to see her I brought a pal along, not because I needed a chaperone, but because Kandi said she lived with a girlfriend.

We had dinner; we talked; we laughed; my buddy and I left. Nothing happened, just fun among friends. Beyond her sensuous beauty, I saw that Kandi had character and class. She was a wonderful listener, a sympathetic soul.

Shortly afterwards, we were playing Leo's Casino in Cleveland when Kandi showed up. I was glad. Whether it was frustration from our unsuccessful pregnancies or the fact that I'd been with Claudette since we were fourteen—I was now twenty-seven—I felt myself moved. I also heard myself telling Kandi that, no matter what, I loved my wife and had no intention of leaving her. At the same time, I wanted Kandi, wanted her as badly as I'd ever wanted any woman. You see, she was both witty and candid. She was easy to be with, as though I'd known her for years. At the same time, she had perfect diction and superb enunciation.

"You're the only black chick I've ever met," I told her, "who talks like the product of a white finishing school."

"Well, I'm interested in acting so I try to speak correctly. But if you want me to, brother, I can get right on down with my street talk, you know."

We laughed. We talked all night and, at five in the morning, though she was very reluctant, I talked her into making love. It was beautiful.

"I just want you to be happy," she said afterwards.

"Do you think a man can be happy with more than one woman?" I asked Daddy Five.

I was back at the house on Belmont. Daddy was up in his room, sipping V.O., talking to me while fixing one of the kids' toys.

"I don't look at it that way, boy," he said. "I look at it like this. Go back to raw times. Before all the rules and regulations. In raw times the natural thing was for a man to have as many women as he wanted—and could afford. That was true in every tribe. The Lord made more women than men. Now you don't expect that He wanted those extra women to go without a man. No, sir. I think He meant for the men to be shared by the women. Look at nature. You see a cow pasture with twenty-five heifers and one bull. He'll kill any other bull who comes close to his heifers. Look at horses. For every thirty mares, you'll see one stallion. Look in the barnyard. For every rooster, there'll be two dozen hens.

"Now one day a woman comes along. A strong woman. And she starts talkin' 'bout, 'Let's cut out this shit. Let's just have one woman for one man.' Hearing that, maybe her man whips her ass, but the next woman who comes along is smarter. She knows she can't win with brawn, so she uses her brain. Says, 'I'm going to make this dude think this is what *he* wants.' See, she plays with his mind. She gets him to marry her. And that starts the whole thing. This civilization business is here to stay, boy, but I don't think it's natural.

Men are always gonna act like they acted in raw times. Most times, one woman per man don't seem to be enough."

Five's philosophy had a powerful influence on me. Though my views would change over the years, to a large degree I agreed with Daddy. I felt that, because of my love and respect for women, I could maintain relationships with more than one. I even fantasized about having children with women of every race and color, all of us living together in one house filled with peace, harmony and happiness.

But I also knew that I was living in the United States of America, where the rule—unlike Europe—was strict fidelity. I never stopped loving Claudette; I wanted to protect her, to avoid hurting her, to keep my thing with Kandi out of her face.

Complicating the situation even more, Claudette met a man who profoundly changed our lives, adding such emotion to our daily drama that I felt like, all things considered, I was living in a soap opera.

All My Children

As a teenager I'd run home to watch those fifteen-minute black-and-white episodes of *The Guiding Light* and *Search for Tomorrow*. Later in my life I'd get hooked on *General Hospital, All My Children* and *One Life to Live*. I've always loved soaps, losing myself in the stories, identifying with the characters, savoring the endless twists and turns of the plots.

Meanwhile, our family plot was developing in a different direction:

"There's a man I want us to meet," said Claudette over breakfast one morning. "His name is Throckmorton, and he's a doctor. He specializes in helping women with problem pregnancies. I've heard he has unusual theories and methods, but I want to see what he's about."

I agreed to accompany her, and a week later we were seated across from a tall, thin elderly gentleman with snow-white hair and kind blue eyes. He had the disheveled mannerisms of an absentminded professor. At the same time, he spoke slowly and thoughtfully, carefully weighing each word while tapping a sharpened pencil on his desk calendar.

"My examination reveals that the shape of your uterus,

Mrs. Robinson, may not support a fetus. The average uterus is heart-shaped and closed at the cervix. Yours is pear-shaped and somewhat open. Your history shows that you have no problem with fertilization. The problem is carrying the fetus to term. I don't see any traditional way to solve that dilemma. Now I don't know either of you, and before I go on, I must ask whether you would consider a rather radical approach to childbirth."

Claudette and I looked at each other. We didn't know what he was talking about.

"Please explain what you have in mind," Claudette answered.

"Implantation."

"What's that?" I wanted to know.

"An experimental method that works like this. You, Mr. Robinson, would impregnate your wife. I would then surgically remove the fertilized egg from her and place it in the womb of another woman, who would carry the child for the full term of pregnancy."

We were shocked—didn't know what to say, didn't know what to think.

"Has this ever been tried before?" Claudette asked.

"There have been a few experiments, but, as far as I'm concerned, this would be my first attempt."

"What are the chances of success?" Claudette inquired.

"Candidly speaking, not good."

"And what about the woman?" I wanted to know. "How could we be guaranteed she wouldn't change her mind and want to keep the baby?"

"We'll have to find the right woman. That will be my responsibility."

"It sounds a little crazy," I said, my head spinning.

"If you agree," Throckmorton continued, "I'll have to

closely monitor Mrs. Robinson's ovulations. Through a strict vitamin and food regimen, we'll also build up your sperm count. Moreover, it's essential that this entire procedure remain undisclosed. The laws do not yet recognize my methods. If discovered, I could easily lose my license."

"What about after the baby's born?" I asked. "What do we tell people?"

"The truth—that the baby's adopted, because that's exactly what you'll have to do."

"If you yourself could get into trouble," Claudette remarked, "why are you risking this?"

"Because, my child," he said, taking off his rimless professorial glasses and looking her square in the eye, "I think I'm right."

Claudette and I talked about it all afternoon; we were up all that night. It seemed so bizarre, transferring an egg from one woman to another. The hush-hush atmosphere didn't help matters. What if Throckmorton was a fraud? Yet he seemed so sincere and scientific. Meanwhile, we still wanted a baby more than ever. After the death of the twins, we desperately wanted to avoid the heartache of another miscarriage. But the chances of this experiment working weren't all that good either.

What should we do?

"Doo," said Claudette, "I say we try."

"I'm willing," I agreed.

And so we did.

Throckmorton was delighted. Like a scientist about to embark on a bold experiment, he was energized by the challenge. He was so enthusiastic about our decision, he offered us prenatal and hospital services free of charge. I also think, in a purely fatherly way, he fell for Claudette. She was his pet patient.

Then the waiting began.

Months after we first met with him, he finally called to say that he'd found a willing woman.

"All she asks," he said, "is that you pay her college tuition."

I gladly agreed.

The egg was taken from Claudette and implanted in the surrogate mother. Then more waiting, weekly reports from Throckmorton, hoping, worrying, praying . . .

In March of 1968 he called to say that the woman was entering her second trimester of pregnancy.

"All indications are that she'll carry the fetus full term," Throckmorton declared. "If I were you, I'd start telling my friends and relatives that you and Mrs. Robinson have applied for adoption."

We celebrated that night, thrilled at the thought of becoming parents at last. We also decided that we would each tell one close friend the absolute truth. I told Berry and Claudette told Earlyn, Ronnie White's wife. We told everyone else that we were hoping to adopt a girl.

The call came on August 16, 1968.

"I'm happy to say," announced Throckmorton, "that you are parents of a healthy baby boy."

We explained to our friends that the adoption agency had urged us to adopt a baby boy who had just arrived and bore an uncanny resemblance to me.

Legally, we adopted the child the day after his birth— how strange to adopt your own baby!—and called him Berry William Borope Robinson—Berry after Berry Gordy, William after me, and Borope after the first two letters of my partners' names: Bobby, Ronnie and Pete.

Looking at my son for the first time, I couldn't contain myself; I wept as though I were the baby. I thanked God for the gift of his life, and the dedicated doctor who was midwife to the miracle.

"What do you think?"

"I think he's beautiful."

"Do you think he looks like me?"

"Exactly."

"You think people will think I had him with another woman?"

"I don't think you care what people think. I think you're just happy to have him."

"You're right," I said, kissing Kandi.

I'd brought little Berry to her apartment so she could see him. He was only a month old—normal, strong and healthy, everything a father could ask for.

Kandi held him in her arms, caressed his cheeks, kissed his tiny hands. She was so happy for me, her eyes filled with tears. Then she broke the news.

"I'm going away."

"What!"

"I'm leaving Detroit."

"Why?"

"It isn't fair. You and Claudette finally have what you've always wanted. I couldn't live with myself if I did anything to destroy that. I'm a distraction. I love you too much, I have too much respect for Claudette to damage your life together."

"Where are you going?"

163

"They've offered me a job at the Playboy Club in San Francisco. I've accepted."

I wanted to stop her, wanted to argue, wanted to convince her to stay. But reason wasn't on my side. What did I have to offer Kandi? She had my love; I genuinely cared for her, but the commitment wasn't there. The commitment was reserved for my family. She knew—and I knew too—that her future wasn't with me. I kissed her long and hard that afternoon. Kissed her and made her promise to stay in touch. After all, we were friends.

Carrying Berry to the car, turning to wave to her one last time, I knew she was doing the right thing. I also knew that, given the strength of our attraction, it'd be hell for us to stay apart. And I wondered, *Would it really be possible?*

A week later, on a hot Sunday afternoon, Daddy Five and I were at Tiger Stadium watching Mickey Lolich mow down the Indians. This was little Berry's first ball game. It was also the year Detroit would win the World Series, beating Cleveland to the pennant by sixteen and a half games.

Daddy was already trying to turn little Berry into an Indian fan.

"No use," I said. "He's too smart to root for a loser."

"You talk that shit, boy, and he'll believe you. Listen to your grandpa," Daddy declared, putting Berry on his lap. "Cleveland's your team, and don't you forget it."

"Listen, Daddy," I said, changing subjects, "people say a man can't be in love with two women at the same time. What do you think?"

"I think what people say doesn't mean diddly squat. Only thing that matters is what you feel. Nobody can tell you who you love or who you don't love. You know your own heart."

I took a bite out of a hamburger while Daddy bounced Berry on his knee. I stared aimlessly as Jim Northrup flied out to left field.

"Thinking about Kandi?" he asked me.

Daddy knew her, just like I had known his women when I was a kid. In fact, Kandi even called him Daddy.

"Thinking about everything," I answered.

"Let her go, boy," he said. "Just let the girl go."

Letting Go

The air was clear. From Berry Gordy's home in the Hollywood Hills, the one he'd just bought from Tommy Smothers, you could see for miles. Below, the Los Angeles basin seemed so vast, a mad matrix of freeways and boulevards, porn shops and movie studios, mansions and shacks.

"Look to your right, Smoke," said Berry. "You can see the ocean."

In the distance the Pacific shimmered under the morning sun.

Claudette had gone inside to feed little Berry. We'd come out to California to show big Berry his godson.

After pointing out a few more sights, Berry got down to business.

"I've decided to move out here."

"I thought you'd be going back and forth."

"That was the original plan. But, Smoke, I'm telling you, man, this is the place. I love the weather, I love the L.A. attitude, and, as far as business goes, it's all happening here. So much is going on in L.A. Movies, for instance."

"You're going to make movies?"

"I'm going to try."

"You can make movies in Detroit."

"You can make movies in Des Moines if you have to, but movies are made in Hollywood."

"I think it's a mistake, Berry."

"Why?"

"Detroit's your home and your heart. It all happened for you in Detroit. I can't see you leaving."

"I can't see me staying. And I can't see you staying either."

"Forget it, man." I was adamant. "I'm not about to move out here."

"Just think about it, Smoke. All I'm asking you is to consider the idea."

Back inside the house, we were still debating the issue when a messenger arrived with a tape from Detroit.

"From Stevie," said Berry, putting it on.

We sat back and listened to an early version of "Signed, Sealed, Delivered I'm Yours."

The minute it was over, Berry jumped up, all smiles; he couldn't contain himself; just like that, he called Stevie in Detroit.

"Man," he said, "you really pitched a bitch! This jam's a monster!"

I couldn't hear what Stevie said, but Berry's reply was plain. "I don't care if it is a sample mix, that's the mix that's going out. Don't touch it, man. Just get it out there—and I mean *now!*"

The sample mix went out and the song went number one.

Back home, I wasn't happy with my career. I didn't just dislike the traveling; I hated it. Maybe it was the birth of

Berry, maybe it was Kandi leaving, but I was determined to devote myself to my family. Running in and out of town was driving me nuts. And, for the first time, there was also dissension among the troops.

For years I'd tried to supplement the Miracles' income by having them help me compose. If they worked a writing session with me—whether I used their ideas or not—I put their names on the tunes and, consequently, they enjoyed extra earnings. But I also wanted them to write among themselves, hoping they'd generate even more hits. That would lessen their need for live-performance money. It'd mean less pressure on me to tour with the guys.

I didn't really need the concert money. My own situation had steadily improved. I had writer's royalties coming in and also a vice president's salary. The Miracles, though, were reluctant to write without me. And then things got bad between me and Pete Moore.

Pete and I had been inseparable since we were kids, but when he married I found out his wife started whispering shit in his ear. "Smokey's making more than you. . . . Smokey's taking more than he should. . . . Smokey has this and Smokey has that. . . ." Over time, Pete's attitude soured. He started angling against me, doing stuff behind my back.

I was shocked. I was also pissed. After all, he'd known his wife very briefly, but we'd been friends since childhood. Male friendships are sacred to me. I'm just as tight today with my neighborhood buddies—guys I've known since I was five—as I was forty years ago. I'd never let anyone turn me against Pete, and I resented the fact that he let his wife poison his mind.

Then I started contemplating: Because I made more

money than the other guys, I'd always picked out and paid for the group's clothes. I kept us clean, kept us sharp, did lots of extra shit I didn't have to. More and more, I was feeling used and unappreciated.

I confronted Pete with my feelings, but by then the damage had been done. He didn't deny anything, but he didn't really want to talk about it.

In 1969, I decided to quit the Miracles and get the hell off the road. It was no easy decision because, after all, we'd been together most of our lives. In fact, Bobby Rogers and I were born in the same hospital on the same day. If they hadn't put me in the wrong-color nursery, you could say we've been chirping and crying together from the first minutes we popped into the world.

No matter, my peace of mind was slowly being destroyed, and I knew it was time to leave.

"I love you guys," I told them at a meeting at Ronnie White's house, "we're brothers. We'll always be brothers. But there's a time when even brothers have to go their separate ways."

They heard me, my words were clear, but the reality of my decision didn't quite register with them.

Four years before, our name had been changed from the Miracles to Smokey Robinson and the Miracles. It was Berry's idea. He argued that having the leader's name out front would boost business. The guys might have resented it, but they saw his reasoning and said nothing. This time, once again, they quietly accepted what I was saying. Only later did I learn that they didn't believe me.

I'm not sure I believed it myself, because somehow I didn't leave in 1969, or in 1970, or even in 1971. In 1972, I was still touring with the Miracles.

Part of the reason goes back to that Hitsville Christmas party with Stevie Wonder.

Three years after we'd released "The Tears of a Clown," the song I'd written with Stevie, a Motown executive in London decided it had hit potential and put it out in the U.K. After two weeks the thing jumped to number one. Soon it was selling big in five European countries. Finally, in 1970, it was rereleased in America, where it soared to the top of the charts. Turned out to be the Miracles' biggest record ever, selling some three million copies. That was great. But it also put me in a bind.

As a group we were hotter than ever; our performance fee zoomed to $25,000 a night, big money back then.

"Come on, Smoke," my partners pulled on me. "You've got to tour for another year. We need time to get ourselves financially straight."

I agreed. I toured, but I hated it, hated it every time I left the house, hated the cabs and the limos and the planes, hated the hotels and the hotel food, hated the hassles and headaches over equipment and musicians and luggage and sound checks.

When we got to San Francisco, I called Kandi. I'd been worried about her because, on the phone, she'd told me about her stormy affair with Huey Newton of the Black Panthers. There'd been violence, and she was so afraid that for a while she'd gone into hiding.

She came to the Miyako Hotel, saying that Huey was no longer a problem. For three days and three nights, despite our resolve to end our relationship, we stayed together. I realized that, no matter how deep my love for Claudette, I also loved Kandi.

We confided in one another; we escaped into each other's

arms. I sympathized, thinking of my own marriage as Kandi explained how doctors had told her she could never have a child; she listened as I ventilated my frustrations about the tedium and travails of the road.

Kandi was always cool. If she came to the gig, she did so as an ordinary fan. She'd never hang on me or bring attention to herself.

In much the same way, Claudette was cool. We had an unspoken understanding. Maybe it was because, having traveled as a Miracle, Claudette knew how men acted. If, for example, she flew out to see me perform, she'd always call first. She'd never show up unannounced. When she arrived at my hotel, she'd ring my room from the lobby. "Hi, honey," she'd say, "I'll be up in a few minutes." I respected her for being wise enough to avoid the possibility of walking in on anything.

Claudette, a smart and wonderful woman, wanted to maintain our marriage. So did I. I just wanted this Miracles tour to end. I wanted to be back in Detroit.

My desire doubled when I learned that Dr. Throckmorton had called.

"What does he want?" I asked Claudette.

"He says it's too complicated to discuss on the phone. We need to see him in person. This time, he says, he has a whole new approach."

I flew home in a hurry.

Brace Yourself

Sitting in his office, I noticed how, in the past year, Throckmorton had aged. But even though his pale skin was wrinkled and his lanky body bent over, fire still danced in his eyes when he discussed his experiments. He was a man driven to help women have children, and was especially devoted to Claudette.

"I've been studying your problem for years," he told us, "and I think I have another solution."

"Is this one legal?" I joked.

"This one," he said, smiling, "is as legal as the United States Treasury. Please take a look at this."

Slowly, he got up from his desk and placed a large diagram on an easel.

"What is it?" I asked.

"Claudette's uterus."

Again, he went through the heart-shaped versus pear-shaped explanation, showing how her cervix would collapse under pressure.

"But now," he said, his eyes twinkling, "I think we have the solution."

He flipped over the diagram. Beneath it was another sheet of paper, another strange-looking drawing.

"As you can see," Throckmorton declared, "this is a brace, a brace, I must say, of my own design. Isn't it beautiful?"

"What will it do?" asked Claudette.

"It will brace your cervix. It will permit you, my dear lady, to carry and bear your own child."

"Will it work?" I wanted to know.

"I'll do everything I can," Throckmorton promised, "to make sure it works. I just hope I have enough time."

"What do you mean?" Claudette asked.

Turning his eyes away from us, he didn't answer. But I knew what he meant; I could see that, despite his determination, Dr. Throckmorton was a very sick man.

Claudette's pregnancy was thrilling but frustrating for me. She seemed to be getting bigger and stronger, yet I was touring with the Miracles at a madcap pace. We were having our best career year ever. I was miserable or happy, hopeful or despondent, carefree or cranky, depending on whether I was home or on the road.

Making matters worse, Berry stayed on my case about moving to L.A., but I was determined to stay in Detroit. I fought him tooth and nail. Even mailed him a mountain of books on air pollution and earthquakes.

"It's all about to fall in the ocean," I'd tell him on the phone.

"If this sucker falls, I'm falling with it. This is the place, Smoke. I'm here to stay."

"And I'm about to buy a house in Southfield."

Claudette and I had found a beautiful home in the suburbs

outside Detroit with a yard big enough for a couple of holes of golf.

"Don't do it, man," warned Berry. "You'll be making a mistake. You'll be out here before you know it."

"I'll be working out of the Detroit office," I insisted. "This is still where the music's being made."

We'd kept the old Hitsville studio but bought a big building on Woodward Avenue.

"Wait till you hear the music we're making in L.A.," Berry said. "It's hot enough to burn your ass."

The truth is that the first songs Berry produced in California were history-setting hits, four straight smashes on the Jackson Five—"I Want You Back," "ABC," "The Love You Save" and "I'll Be There."

Bobby Taylor, a dynamite singer, had discovered the group in the late sixties and brought them to our attention. Bobby took care of them for a while. In fact, little nine-year-old Michael used to love to ride in the golf cart when Bobby and I were out on the links.

Michael was a strange and lovely child. I always saw him as an old soul in the body of a boy. Jesus is my guide and my joy, but I also believe in reincarnation, contrary to the belief of most Christians. Being with Michael, you felt like he'd lived other lives, he seemed so old to be so young. He was also an astute student. He'd be listening and watching the other acts like a hawk, always learning. His main teachers were Jackie Wilson and James Brown; he had their moves down clean; but it was clear that this kid had dance designs of his own. He was driven, determined, intense, the biggest talent we'd seen since Diana. And the accompaniment of his brothers, bad-ass singers and dancers themselves, only added to the appeal.

Berry headed a production group called the Corporation. He worked with Freddie Perren, Fonce Mizzell and Deke Richards in putting out those early records.

Watching Berry in the studio—just as I had done ten years earlier—Michael got his first lessons in song production. Meanwhile, Motown got its first West Coast hits. I didn't want to admit it, but it seemed like all the signs were pointing to California.

"Things are moving ahead much as I planned," Dr. Throckmorton told us in the first week of December 1970. Our due date was Christmas.

In October he'd put Claudette in the hospital for observation. He saw that the brace needed bolstering, another delicate procedure, which he managed flawlessly.

Now he'd just examined Claudette in his office and was pleased. When he spoke, though, I knew something was wrong—not with her, but with him. His voice was shaky and his eyes bloodshot. He looked sick, but still determined. After all, seeing Claudette give birth had been a burning goal of his for years.

"Since I've always anticipated performing a Caesarian section," he said, "I'm going to recommend that you check into the hospital tomorrow. I'd like to operate as soon as possible."

"Why?" I asked. "What's wrong?"

"It's not the baby. The baby's strong. I just don't know how long my own strength will last. I want to act now, before it's too late."

But it was too late. That night Throckmorton collapsed and was taken to the hospital himself. Understandably, we were afraid—not only for him, but for our unborn child. After all, the brace was Throckmorton's creation. Who else could maneuver this birth? Who else knew the intricacies of Claudette's anatomy?

The phone rang early the next morning. It was Throckmorton, whispering so softly we could barely hear.

"Check into the hospital today . . ." he told Claudette, ". . . just as we planned . . . I'll be able to do it . . . I promise . . . I will not let you down . . ."

But how could he do it from his sickbed? How could he possibly operate?

We found out when we arrived at the hospital: Throckmorton had arranged to hook up a speakerphone in the delivery room. Though he was too weak to get out of bed, and certainly too weak to operate, he could still talk, and his plan was to give directions to the doctors delivering our baby.

He did so—this was Throckmorton's bravest and finest hour—and on December 15, Tamla Claudette Robinson was born, a gorgeous girl, another miracle child.

A week later, his mission accomplished, the good doctor died a peaceful death.

Playing with our beautiful baby, praising God for our bountiful blessings, we remembered him in our prayers— and we still do—as a rare and loving spirit.

Our family was complete. We had a boy and a girl, a fine home in the suburbs, a wonderful housekeeper named Lily Hart. Miss Lily, who'd worked for Motown, had been asked by Berry, as a gracious present, to help us after little Berry's birth. We grew so close, I called her Mama Three.

Now I really wanted to stay home.

"This is it, guys," I said in early 1971. "No more Miracles for me. I don't want my kids not knowing they have a father. I don't want to come home and have them asking me for my autograph."

"But, Smoke," they argued back, "we don't have anyone to replace you."

"Isn't it a little late to be thinking about that shit now? I gave you ample notice."

"We just need a little more time."

"Find a singer, and do it soon, 'cause my patience is shot."

They held auditions, got cats from all over the country, and finally decided on Billy Griffin. Billy was good, but everyone insisted that I had to help him; I had to go on one more extended tour, just to introduce Billy to the public. It'd be our farewell tour. How could I say no?

I couldn't.

Meanwhile, with Motown split between Detroit and L.A., things seemed scattered. I felt scattered. Musically, I was in a holding pattern.

Inspiration finally came, but when it did its source was a shock to everyone.

Dad Does It

"I don't like it," said Berry, back in Detroit for a week of work. "It's not commercial. I don't think they're going to play it on the radio."

"Look, man," I told him. "All the writers and artists love it. We think it's brilliant."

"I'm trying to talk him out of it," Berry said.

"That's like trying to talk a bear out of shittin' in the woods. Dad ain't budging."

In 1971, against the advice of the sales department, Motown released *What's Going On*, Marvin Gaye's masterpiece, the greatest album, in my opinion, ever made by anyone.

Marvin surprised us. Marvin seduced us with a new sound, funky as all hell, that soared with spirituality. He sang about the vicious Vietnam war, the woes in the ghetto, police brutality, drug addiction and the love of God. He stirred up this stew in one hot pot and kept it boiling. Effortlessly, he flowed from theme to theme, one song melting into another. It was the first concept album, the first time I'd ever heard a singer multitrack his voice—answering himself, echoing himself, harmonizing himself—setting a standard for us all to follow.

What's Going On was a sacred work. It also sold like crazy.

The album produced three top-ten singles—the title track, plus "Inner City Blues" and "Mercy Mercy Me"—proving our marketing men mistaken. Most important, though, Dad took our company out of the age of the producer and into the age of the artist. He made musical history.

"The album," explained Marvin, "wasn't done by me, Smoke. It was done by God."

People have pointed to this episode as an example of Motown stifling its artists. The truth is that Berry, though he was the boss, lost the fight—and lost it like a gentleman. He realized with Marvin, and later with Stevie, that these were artists who required freedom. And he gave it to them.

My own case was different. I'd been my own producer from the get-go, so there were no battles to be fought. Motown, like most companies, had been a reflection of the man on top. That man was a producer. As a producer—first, in fact, as my producer—Berry had enjoyed unprecedented success. His protégés—Holland-Dozier-Holland, Norman Whitfield, myself—followed in his footsteps. In the sixties the Motown artists were happy to be produced; they were delighted to have a chance to be directed.

By the start of the seventies, though, many of those artists —most noticeably Marvin—had learned to produce themselves. They no longer needed instruction or direction. They were capable of creating their own finished product.

It was Motown, so often criticized for fencing in artists, that tore down the fences. Marvin did it magnificently with *What's Going On*; a year later Stevie broke through with *Talking Book*. My artistic break wouldn't come until the mid-seventies. I felt Marvin's mighty influence, but I still hadn't cut the cord with the Miracles.

First I'd have to make it through our Farewell Tour, a time of turbulence and tears.

Coasting

Berry didn't lay off.

He likes to tease as much as me. And like me, he doesn't like losing.

That same Christmas after the birth of Tamla—named, by the way, after the Motown subsidiary for which we'd recorded—Berry called from L.A.

"How's the baby?" he asked.

"Beautiful," I said. "You should see her."

"I want to, but I can't get out there for a while. I hear the airport's closed and you're buried under ten feet of snow."

"It's a little rough," I said, wind howling and sleet slamming against the side of the house.

"I got those books you sent me, the ones about the earthquake. Real nice of you, Smoke."

"Don't mention it, man."

"Wait a minute," he suddenly said, "... this chick over here is splashing me ... stop splashing, baby ... get out of the pool ... and don't forget to put on some sun lotion, sugar ... with that tiny bikini you got on, I don't want your body getting burned ... now what were you saying, Smoke? Is it still snowing back there?"

*   *   *

Six weeks later, on the morning of February 10, me and the Miracles arrive on the Dallas–L.A. red-eye.

The Four Tops have been touring Texas with us—we're extremely close friends with the Tops—and, right after the gig, we all decide to fly out to California, our next concert stop.

Check into the Century Plaza Hotel at 3:30 a.m. At 5:30, I wake up, tossing and turning. I can't sleep. I wonder why. Ordinarily I'd be out till noon. But this morning has me anxious and agitated. Something's wrong.

At 6 a.m., it hits.

Rumbling, rolling, shaking, quaking, pitching, my room's coming apart, the hotel's quivering like Jell-O. From the balcony I look out to see swimming pools thrown up in the air, electric currents hissing and shooting off sparks and fire. Sidewalks are cracking. People are screaming.

This is the Great Los Angeles Earthquake of 1971.

All the hotel guests, scared out of their wits, congregate in the lobby. Now here comes Levi Stubbs wearing his pj's and carrying his suitcase and talkin' 'bout, "Man, I'm getting the hell out of here!"

"We got some dates to play in L.A.," I reminded him. "You can't go nowhere."

"The hell I can't. I'll commute."

Even though the situation is serious, we can't help but laugh at Levi.

For days after, the hotel's rumbling from aftershocks. To kill time, we play cards and have killer chess tournaments —the Miracles versus the Tops. But with every new little shake or quake, Levi jumps up and runs to the door.

"I can't take this shit, man. I gotta get out of here."

We fall on the floor laughing.

Three days later, with the phones finally repaired, a call comes in from Berry.

"Hey, Smoke," he says, "welcome to L.A."

"Say, man, where you been?"

"In Freeport, the Bahamas. Been here for a week. Wish you could see it. Damn, it's beautiful!"

"You mean you missed the earthquake?"

"You felt it for me. You'll give me all the details when I get home. Meanwhile, stay cool, Smoke," he laughs.

During the last tour with the Miracles, my mood changed from bad to worse. I played dates with them, introducing Billy Griffin as the new lead singer, well into the summer of 1972. I felt like a prisoner in a cage of my own making. I knew what it meant to be a lame-duck President. My Miracle thing had been dead for years; yet here I was, still performing, still trying to act like my heart was in it.

The last gig was a heavy happening. I decided to film my final day with the Miracles, from playing chess and cards in the dressing room to the concert that night at the Carter Barron Ampitheater in Washington, D.C. Junior Walker was opening for us, but it rained so hard and long into the evening, with flashing lightning and booming thunder, that Junior had to be canceled. Dramatically, the downpour stopped at ten o'clock, just in time for us to go on. A loyal capacity crowd had braved the storm. They were waiting for us.

Back in my dressing room, I'd been despondent and guilty, I guess, over leaving the guys.

Beans Bowles was our musical director, Taylor Cox our manager and Jimmy Johnson, the cat we called Mother, our

road manager. They were consoling me, being both philosophical and fatherly.

"You've given to the guys, Smoke," said Beans.

"You've overgiven," Mother maintained.

I went out onstage and, though I'd been trying to quit for
years, a sadness suddenly engulfed me, an awesome feeling of
loss and regret. I was being bubbly for the fans, singing and
dancing, but I was dying on the inside, feeling like the character
in "The Tears of a Clown," smiling through my pain. I hated the
thought that I'd never be onstage with these guys again; I hated
the notion of singing the last song. I tried to avoid it; I kept on
singing, singing for over two hours until Ronnie White came
over and whispered, "Smoke, it's time to wrap it up."

Our last song was "Going to a Go Go." Then we were gone.

Backstage, we were all crying for real, hugging and holding one another.

"I just wish you guys well," was all I could say, over and
over again, realizing how much they meant to me and how
much I'd miss them.

"I don't know how long I'll stay with them, Smoke," said
Marv Tarplin. "I'll just have to see."

"You're doing the right thing, man. You've got to give it
a try."

I tried to fall asleep that night, but couldn't, my mind
crowded with over two decades of memories—singing on
street corners, dance hops, hayrides, skating rinks, the Five
Chimes, the Matadors, the Miracles.

I knew that my life, for better or worse, would never be
the same.

PART FOUR

Solo

The Major Move

The chapter was closed. I was out of the Miracles. It was June of 1972, and I could finally enjoy some peace of mind. For fourteen years I'd been running around—writing, producing, performing. Now I just wanted to kick back and be with the beautiful kids that Claudette and I had struggled so hard to have.

I was retired, in Southfield, Michigan, a man devoted to his family and the noble game of golf. Just to make sure I didn't get flabby, I also started a long-distance-running routine.

My retirement was sweet for as long as it lasted—a month.

"We can't talk about it anymore, Smoke," said Berry on the long-distance wire. "If you want to go on with Motown, you're going to have to move to L.A. And to tell you the truth, I can't see you doing anything else. I can't see us *not* working together. You've always been a part of this company. I've always counted on your input, man, and these days I need it more than ever. I need you out here. Now."

Berry had just made *Lady Sings the Blues* with Diana Ross, Billy Dee Williams and Richard Pryor. The movie would prove to be a big hit—I'd get to name and write the lyrics to Michel

Legrand's lush theme song, "Happy"—but it hadn't opened yet and Berry, who'd poured his own money in the production, was nervous.

I could feel how the pressure of moviemaking was getting to Berry. It was one thing to deal with the record business. But now he was up against cold-blooded cutthroat smack-you-down hope-you-fail Hollywood. Beyond my job as vice president—which mainly meant screening and signing new talent—I had a feeling Berry simply needed my friendship. At the same time, it still hurt when I thought of leaving Detroit.

That Sunday, me and Daddy Five did something we hadn't done for twenty-five years. We went on the Boblo boat ride. I took little Berry along—Tamla stayed home with Claudette —so he could experience what I'd experienced as a kid.

He loved it, just as I'd loved it—this big ol' three-deck ferry boat sloshing up and down the Detroit River, folks from the neighborhood toting beer and chicken, ribs and melon and sweet-potato pie. There was dancing and flirting, lots of loud laughing, whiskey bottles hidden in brown paper bags, generations of friends and family, a special mellow floating picnic on a warm summer's day.

Felt like I knew everyone aboard, all three hundred passengers. After all, I'd been living in Detroit all my thirty-two years. And Detroit, especially on that Sunday, seemed like nothing more than a big country town.

We were sitting at a table on the top deck, heading downriver, the hot sun putting my son to sleep. The little guy napped in my arms as Five and I shot the shit.

"I've seen you say hello to at least four of your women

on this boat," I teased Daddy. "And I saw you dodging another two."

"Boy, you don't know what you're seeing or what you're saying. Besides, I'm like you, I'm retired."

"Retired from what?"

"Retired from keeping up. If anyone does any chasing these days, it's going to have to be the ladies, not me."

"What would you think about chasing out to California?"

"You moving there?"

"Think I should?"

"Your boss is out there, ain't he? I expect he's missing you pretty bad."

Daddy Five knew what was happening without being told.

"But I hate to leave this," I said. "I hate to leave home."

"Your home is right there in your arms. Your home ain't nothing more than your old lady and your kids."

"What about your home?"

"You ain't gotta worry about me."

"You were the first one to take me to California," I reminded him. "Remember that trip out west?"

Thinking about it, he laughed. "You were looking for Roy Rogers."

"Look, Daddy, I'm telling you right now. If I move out there, you're coming along, whether you like it or not."

"Who said I wouldn't like it?" he asked, smiling through a slow sip of V.O.

That did it. If Daddy came along, I suppose I could stand it.

At first Claudette was reluctant. It wasn't easy for her to consider leaving family and friends, but she went along with the decision. She knew that our future was with Motown, and as far as Detroit went, Motown was long gone.

189

*　　　*　　　*

By August, only two months after I'd left the Miracles, I was living in a hotel on Wilshire Boulevard in Westwood, waiting for Claudette to sell the house and settle our affairs so that she, the kids, Miss Lily and Daddy Five could move out and join me.

Strange, but during the interlude, my heart kept jumping back to the Miracles—not because I wanted to rejoin, but because, despite the discord with Pete at the end, the guys still meant so much to me.

I wrote a song for them called "Sweet Harmony," and before the music began I spoke this introduction over Marv Tarplin's lilting guitar licks:

"This song," I said, "is dedicated to some people with whom I had the pleasure of spending over half the years I've lived till now, when we've come to our fork in the road. And though our feet may travel down different paths, I want them to know how I feel about them, and that I wish them well."

I sang:

Sweet harmony
Go on and blow on
Stay in perfect tune
Through your unfamiliar song
Make the world aware
That you're still going strong, go on,
Spread joy around the world
. . . I believe in miracles
If you can dream it, it can be done
And though a task was made for two
It can be done well by one
Spread joy around the world

Suzanne DePasse, then head of our A&R department, heard the song and loved it. She urged me to put it out on an album.

"But I'm retired," I protested.

"You're retired from performing," she said, "not from writing and singing."

About that same time Marv Tarplin called me from Detroit.

"It's too weird, Smoke. The group's all chiefs and no Indians. Everyone wants to be in charge, and I'm going crazy. I'd rather be out there in California with you."

"Come on out, man."

When he arrived he had a tape of some of the softest, sweetest, most sensitive midnight guitar music I'd ever heard. Pam Moffett helped me with the lyrics and "Baby, Come Close," my first solo single, was also my first solo hit. Along with "Sweet Harmony," I included it on *Smokey,* my debut solo album, coproduced with Willie Hutch and released in 1973.

Though I worked in the studio and the Motown office, I stayed off the road. With this first record, though, my new career was off to a nice start. My concentration stayed on Claudette and the kids. Kandi and I had cooled it. I didn't think I was vulnerable to a new romance.

I was wrong.

As the World Turns

It was turning towards spring.

We'd found a house in Beverly Hills and were living the good life. Claudette had settled in, Daddy Five was tinkering around with the cars in the driveway, Mama Three was in the kitchen, the kids were in nursery school. Little by little, I was adjusting to living under the palm trees and jogging past the homes of movie stars.

It was nine in the morning, and I was cruising, kicking the last leg of my four-mile run down Elevado. It was one of those rare clear L.A. mornings when you could breathe.

"Hey, Smoke!"

I stopped. It was Diana Ross coming out to pick up the newspaper from her front porch. She lived only five blocks from me.

"Hey, baby, what's happening?" I asked her.

"Isn't this something, Smoke, we grew up down the street from each other and here we are again—down the street from each other."

"Yeah, girl, you're still following me around."

She laughed and gave me a big smile. Dressed in a robe and slippers, Diane looked very much like the average house-wife in the morning.

"What are you doing up this early, girl?"

"Shoot, man, I'm a mama now. I've gotta get up. My kids are already yelling for breakfast."

"They do change our lives, don't they?"

"Did you know Berry's thinking about doing another film with me, Smoke? He's already got someone started on the script."

"Is that the *Mahogany* thing he was telling me about?"

"That's it. So much is happening right now—the kids, this movie, designing costumes, recording a new album, and on top of everything, I've been rehearsing night and day 'cause I open in Vegas in a week. It sure would be good if you could be there, Smoke."

The curtain opened and, walking down a stairway in the middle of the orchestra, dressed in a floor-length white mink coat, dazzling diamonds dripping from her ears, diamonds wrapped around her wrists, Diana Ross did not look like the average housewife.

The Caesar's Palace audience went wild. The show was a smash. I was at a booth with Berry, Marvin Gaye and Johnny Bristol. Diana did her "Reach Out and Touch" routine where she walked through the audience and invited her fans to sing. She came to our booth and had Marvin, myself and Johnny each sing a chorus. The crowd loved it. Her closing number was "Ain't No Mountain High Enough."

"Okay, Marvin, I know you know this song," she said. "Get on up here. You too, Smoke. You too, Johnny."

We killed it.

Afterwards, in her dressing room, we had a ball. Dad was glowing because his "Let's Get It On" had gone through the roof. It was one of those rare times he seemed happy to be in show business. Diana was glowing because her solo career was outshining her success with the Supremes. Berry was glowing because he always glows when one of his students excels. That night, three of his students had shown him how his fanatical-motivational schooling had paid off.

I was glowing because I'd had a ball at the show, and, better yet, the Miracles were surviving without me. Their "Do It, Baby" was going to number one. And best of all, my golf game was improving.

Back in L.A., my second solo album, *Pure Smokey*, had been released. I liked it, liked a song I'd written called "The Love Between Me and My Kids," liked the tunes I'd done with Marv Tarplin and my sister Rose Ella, but still didn't have a connecting chord. I was still searching for a new concept.

Things were perking along on a Thursday afternoon as I pulled into the parking lot and went up to my office in the Motown building on Sunset Boulevard. The new *Billboard* magazine showed that our discovery out of Tuskegee, Alabama, the Commodores, had scored their first big hit, "Machine Gun." I was in a merry mood.

"Meta's on the phone," said my secretary over the intercom.

I flashed back to the one and only time I'd met Meta, over a year before:

I'd been the executive producer of the Miracles' first album without me—I still couldn't totally break the tie—and, in that capacity, had taken them to a television studio to do *Soul Train*, the dance show.

On my way out one of the dancers, a young woman, approached me. Stopped me dead in my tracks.

It was something like when, as a child, I had seen Marva Jean my first day of kindergarten. I was suddenly viewing pure, blinding beauty.

"Mr. Robinson," she said, "my name's Meta and I'd like to start a local fan club for you."

Entertainers like being adored or else, I suppose, they wouldn't be entertainers. I'm no different. I'm susceptible, yet I've never liked groupies.

Meta was no groupie. She was a genuine fan who knew my music better than me. She spoke sincerely and intelligently. I also couldn't help but notice her body—a dancer's body—which, top to bottom, was shaped like a sculpture, a work of art. She had big hazel eyes, a creamy mulatto complexion and a perky persistent personality.

"Will it be all right if I call you?" she asked.

"You can call my office," I answered, giving her the number.

She called persistently, and just as persistently I'd avoided speaking to her. At the same time, I hadn't forgotten her—her shape and her smile were fixed in my mind—but, knowing myself, I knew it best to avoid temptation. Today, though, I figured—why not?

"Hey, Meta."

"You're talking to me!" she said in an especially sweet voice. "I'm shocked."

"What have you been doing?" I asked.

"I have a job working with handicapped children."

For some reason I didn't believe her, and told her so.

"Why don't you believe me?"

"You seem too young."

"I just celebrated my twenty-first birthday."

"Still don't believe you."

"Call the agency. Ask for me."

I did. I called this social service agency and, sure enough, Meta had a job there. She'd told me the truth.

"Look," she said, "let's just have lunch."

"You want me to pick you up?" I asked.

"It won't be necessary. I have my own car. Let's meet somewhere."

We met, and, if anything, she appeared more beguiling than I'd remembered. I knew what was happening but I couldn't, I didn't stop myself.

Months went by. We started meeting often, and soon it became more than a powerful physical relationship. I felt myself falling, confused by the feelings I had for Meta and the devotion and affection I still felt for Claudette.

I was in love with Claudette, but had I also fallen in love with Meta?

In raw times, as Daddy Five would say, I'd simply have them both, without worry or guilt. That's man's nature. But these were the years of women's liberation, and as a woman lover, I saw attitudes changing.

Meta was the sort of companion—like Kandi, like Claudette—who was not only smart, but compassionate, kind-hearted, a real friend. Musically, she'd encourage me, offering candid critiques of my compositions. I also thought she was honest until one day she shocked me with a piece of news:

*　　*　　*

In the morning, I'd played the last round of the Music Industry Golf Tournament in Palm Springs, a three-day affair. Now, after an amorous afternoon, Meta and I were heading home. The sun was setting, a gentle desert breeze blowing sweetly. What a moment for lovers . . .

I reached over for Meta's hand when I saw tears in her eyes.

"What's wrong?" I asked.

"Oh, nothing . . ."

"You can't be crying for nothing, honey."

She sighed.

I kept prodding, probing, trying to find the source of the sadness.

Finally, she said, "Look, G.E."—she called me Green Eyes or just G.E.—"there's something I have to tell you."

Oh God, I thought to myself, *she knows I'm never leaving Claudette, so she's found another guy.*

"I haven't been entirely truthful with you," she confessed.

My heart sank.

"I lied to you," said Meta.

Now here comes the ugly truth about this other guy.

"When did you lie?" I asked.

"When I gave you my age. I'm not twenty-one, I'm eighteen."

I was shocked. But it explained many things—why she didn't want me to come by her house, why she didn't want me to meet her mother and family, why she always had to be in at an early hour.

"I'd feel better, Meta," I said, "if I could talk to your mother about it."

198

"Oh no, please don't do that. Mama would never understand. And she just might cause you trouble."

For days I pondered. Disturbed, I twisted and turned at night, and finally, knowing that I wanted Meta in my life, I decided to call her mother.

"I just wanted to say that if I had known your daughter's age," I told Meta's mama, "I would not have dated her."

"It doesn't surprise me that Meta lied about her age," said the tough-talking woman, "because when she wants something, she's very determined. But why are you calling me? Why are you telling me this?"

"I'm not sure . . . it's just . . ."

"You didn't have to call."

"I felt compelled."

"Feels to me like you really care about her."

"Look, can I come and see you?"

"Why?"

"I guess I'd like to explain how I feel—in person."

She agreed, and I met with Meta's mama, just the two of us. She saw I was sincere. She said, "You could have run away from this situation, but you haven't. You've fallen in love with Meta—I can see that—but you also have a wife. Are you sure you know what you're getting yourself into? A situation like this could be very hard on your wife and on my daughter, but especially on you."

I thought of one of my songs. Funny how the lyrics seemed relevant so many years after I'd written them:

Everyday things change
And some old ideas give way to some new
Certain things rearrange
Like the new idea of me being caught by you

What's this whole world coming to?
Things just ain't the same
Anytime the hunter gets captured by the game

We were both having a lousy day on the links—me and Marvin Gaye.

On the way to the golf course, we'd been followed by female fans. It took us awhile to lose them.

Marvin and Anna had moved to L.A. a little after me, though their marriage was stormier than ever. Dad's career was still blazing hot—"Distant Lover" was burning up the charts—but he was as schizoid as ever, bouncing between religion and raunch.

"Met someone who's just blown my mind, Smoke," he said as we teed off, his ball bouncing into a nasty trap.

"Got the same problem, Dad, but I'm fixing to wipe her from my system."

I shanked my ball deep into a grove of bushes.

"How do you wipe a woman from your system?" asked Dad.

"Perseverance," I said. "Mental discipline."

Marvin chuckled, his eyes sliding across his face in definite disbelief.

"Is she younger than Claudette?"

"Yes," I confessed. "But I'm still in love with Claudette. We're spending more time together, having talks, taking walks, making love. I'm doing everything to concentrate on my marriage, man. But that's my story. What's yours? Who's this fine young thing you found, Dad?"

"Janis. Young and gorgeous. There's no resisting."

"I'm going to resist, man," I said. "I'm telling you, I'm absolutely positively forgetting I ever met Meta."

"Why forget?"

"Because I love her too much."

"We're always going to be tested, Smoke," said Dad in his whimsical way, "and we're always going to fail."

I wanted to respond, but I figured I better find my ball first.

"First and foremost," I told Claudette, "I don't want to hurt you."

"You've done that already, Doo."

"I didn't mean to."

"Look, Smokey, save the speeches. Just tell me what you're going to do."

"I'm going to move out."

"Permanently?"

"I don't know. I can't say. All I know is that for months I've tried to forget this woman and I haven't been able to. It's not fair to you."

"Then go."

"You sound so sure of yourself," I said.

"I'm not sure of anything. But I know I can't keep you if you don't want to stay. And I've got too much pride to beg. If you want to be alone and try to find yourself, Smokey, do it. Just get out before I lose my temper. *Get out now!*"

I was out for a year. Lived alone in an apartment. Saw Meta, but also saw Claudette. The more I worked on putting myself together, the more I tore myself apart. Meta was super-fine, a passion, a comfort, a great companion. But Claudette was a woman of dignity and depth. The more I was away

201

from her, the more I loved her, the more I wanted her, the more I kept going back, switching between the two, certain that my feeling for one didn't exclude the other, but uncertain of how it would all end.

Marriage vows were on my mind.

Two of the world's sweetest people—Jermaine Jackson of the Jackson Five and Berry's daughter Hazel Joy—got married. Hazel asked me to write something and sing it at the ceremony. I did.

It was a beautiful wedding, with white doves, fragrant flowers, sumptuous spreads of scrumptious foods.

"We're going to write the book on happiness," I sang, "pages that time cannot erase, starting here and now, from this time and place."

Tears were in my eyes—for young love, old love, love lost and love refound.

Business went on. Much to my dismay, the Miracles decided to disconnect from Motown. On the heels of their two hits, CBS offered them big bucks up front.

"Ab won't match the offer," the boys told me, referring to Motown president Ewart Abner.

"We'll never be able to match the giants for advance money," I told my ex-partners. "But if you go with CBS and don't have a hit, they'll drop you in a minute. You'll be able to record here as long as you want. We're never going to give up on the Miracles."

They left nevertheless. Couldn't resist the cash. Unfortunately, I was right. CBS didn't like their first effort, kept it on the shelf and never really communicated the problem. Slowly but surely, the Miracles were fading out.

*　　　*　　　*

I was fading into my feelings. Trying to see what I wanted and where I belonged.

Eleven months after I'd moved out, I was up at the Beverly Hills house, hanging out with Five and Tamla—I came to visit nearly every day—seeing how she had her ornery grandpa wrapped around her finger.

"You better go up and see little Berry," said Daddy. "He's been looking for you."

I went up to my son's room. By now Berry was seven. We'd grown close, but my leaving had obviously caused a strain.

"Hi, son."

"Daddy," he said, sitting on his bed, having a hard time looking me in the eye. "I feel bad."

"Why should you feel bad, baby?"

"Because I don't feel safe here in the house with you gone. We have the alarm system and Daddy Five is here, but Daddy Five is an old man, and if someone broke into the house, it would be only him and me to protect Mommy and Tamla and Lily."

"Well, son, I don't think anyone's going to break into the house."

"I want you to come home, Daddy." Then he paused before telling me one of the most devastating things I've ever had to hear: "I know you work real hard, Daddy, and that me and Tamla and all our friends make a lot of noise and everything so that's why you moved away because you needed to rest."

I tried explaining to him, but words wouldn't come, I was fighting back tears. Finally, I managed to get out, "No son ..."

"I'll stop making noise, Daddy, I promise I will. I won't

let my friends come over and when I play I'll whisper and tiptoe and you'll never even know I'm playing and you'll be able to sleep and sing and you won't have to live in a different house . . ."

"It's not your fault," I choked, trying to explain to him just as Five, thirty years before, had explained to me.

Berry continued to plead. I sat there and held him. I kissed him and told him that I loved him, that I would always love him.

Then I went into the bathroom and cried my eyes out for an hour. Berry's plea tore me apart.

What was I doing to my children that they thought this was all their fault?

What was I doing to my family, to my wife?

What was I doing to myself?

Downstairs, Claudette was reading in the den. She looked up and saw my reddened eyes.

"If you'll let me in," I said, "I'd like to come back."

Quiet Storm

A butterfly caught up in a hurricane—the image suddenly came to me.

I put the words in the song. I heard distant thunder, smelled the air just before the rain, saw lightning streak across the sky, felt the winds blow.

Soft winds . . . warm breeze . . . a power source . . . a tender force . . . quiet storm . . . blowing through my life . . .

I finally had the musical concept I'd been seeking since hearing Dad's *What's Going On*. I also had a device for moving from one tune to another: the wind. I saw seven songs carried on the back of a breeze, blowing through the record from start to finish.

Quiet Storm, cowritten with my wonderfully creative sister Rose Ella, also expressed something deep inside my soul, a sense of stirring discontent—happy, on one hand, to be home, but anxious, on the other, to start performing.

For the first time in my solo career I went into the studio dead-set determined to come out with a killer album. I wanted a big record. And I got it.

The album was a hit, but, even more, it started a new

radio format, actually called Quiet Storm—soft romantic soul music with a sexy bite.

Soon Quiet Storm stations started popping up all over the country. It pleased me that the acceptance of my *Quiet Storm* album had created a whole category of radio.

In 1975, I was feeling restless. Night after night, I'd go out to nightclubs, checking out acts. If Joe Blow and the Hoola Hoopers were there, I'd show up; I'd go see anyone, thinking, all the while, of how I'd like to be up there singing. I was hungry for the stage; I hadn't performed for three years. I realized that I needed to entertain people, like I needed to eat, to stay alive.

Since coming to L.A., my job definition had changed. I was no longer seeking new talent; I'd become more of a financial administrator.

"I'm sitting up in my office," I told Berry, "signing checks until I feel like a clerk."

"Don't worry about your office, Smoke," he said. "I want you to do what makes you happy. If that means concentrating on your career, do it."

My debut was in a little club in Florida. It felt a little like starting over, although the club was packed to the rafters with well-wishers and supporters like my old friend Barney Ales, no longer with Motown, and his wife, Mitzi.

When I got onstage, I missed looking to my left and seeing Ronnie, Bobby and Pete, smiling and stepping and singing behind me. It felt strange. And to make matters worse, my musical director actually flipped out onstage. He started running through the audience and screaming how Martians were chasing him. I knew this solo shit wasn't going to be easy.

Bad things lead to good, though, 'cause shortly after this gruesome episode, I hooked up with Sonny Burke. He's been my main music man ever since—killer keyboardist, classy conductor, artful arranger, cool coproducer. Burke is bad.

Another quiet storm was brewing inside me. I thought it was time for me to start my own publishing company. Up till then, Jobete, the Motown subsidiary, owned all my music copyrights. Given what Berry had done for me, I thought that was fair. Besides, my writer's royalties had assured me material comfort for the rest of my life. But industry practice was changing. Artists were demanding—and receiving—publishing income from their compositions. And now that I was giving up most of my corporate duties for my career, I wanted to start accumulating my own valuable copyrights, not only for myself, but as an inheritance for my children. That's why I decided to name my publishing firm Bertam, for little Berry and Tamla.

First I discussed it with Barney Ales, who'd rejoined the company as president.

"See Berry," he said. "He's the only one who can give the okay."

By now Berry had moved from the Hollywood Hills to an even more spectacular spread high in the hills of Bel Air. His place was palatial.

On an overcast morning Barney and I waited for him in his den. He was unusually late. When he finally showed up I could see he was uptight.

"Berry," I said, "I really think it's time for me to publish my own songs."

He was distracted by a barrage of phone calls, and I wasn't sure if he'd heard what I had said.

"Berry," I repeated, "this is important to me. I want to start keeping my own copyrights."

"I wish you wouldn't bother me with this piddly shit right now, Smoke. I'm in the middle of making a movie and—"

"It's not piddly to me, Berry."

"Look, you can have your publishing, you can have anything you want, but leave me alone 'cause I don't have time for it."

With that he got up and left me and Barney sitting in the room. I was stung, disappointed, pissed. I looked at Barney. He shrugged. What could he say? Berry was my best friend and here he was, treating me like dirt.

Fuck the motherfucker, I thought, walking out the door.

I thought about the encounter for weeks; it haunted me, it bugged the shit out of me, but slowly I began to understand. I learned, for instance, that Berry had just fired the director of his new film, *Mahogany*, and taken over that responsibility himself. I also heard that he and Diana were at each other's throats. Their professional relationship, I believe, had been complicated not only by her marriage but by her growing desire for professional independence. No wonder the cat was uptight.

I waited a few months before bringing it up again.

An opening came when, one day, he dropped by my house to see the kids. We were sitting in the backyard when I said, "Man, you really got me upset."

"When?"

"When I mentioned my own publishing company."

208

"But I approved it. You made your deal, didn't you?"

"I made it, but you acted like you were doing me a favor. You nearly bit my head off. But it's okay, because after thinking about it, I finally understood what you were going through, and I know it must have been hell for you."

He got up, grabbed me out of my chair and hugged me hard. "That wasn't me, man. That was some Hollywood asshole trying to get a movie made. Look, you're my person for life. If this ship ever goes down, you and me will be holding on to each other till the bitter end, just like we were holding on to each other at the beginning. It's you and me, Smoke, today, tomorrow and for the rest of the set."

For the rest of the year, my quiet storm subsided. But then, I have to admit, it blew up again. Though I was back home with Claudette, my relationship with Meta hadn't run its course.

Meta inspired me. I couldn't let go of her. She was with me nearly every night when I recorded the *Quiet Storm* album; she was, in fact, the quiet storm I felt blowing through my life. She aroused me, stirring my songs, heightening my art.

I wrote about it:

What's it all about, this crazy love?
How did our two worlds entwine?
How do I fit into your life?
How do you fit into mine?

Love like ours is never ever free
You pay some agony for the ecstasy

Meta knew, though, that I'd never leave my wife for another woman. She also knew that, if she saw me, it'd have to be on that basis. I told her that I could never give her my full romantic attention. Prime time belonged to Claudette. I felt guilty. I wish I could have made up my mind to be with one or the other. I felt like a tennis ball. Claudette and Meta were both rackets; my emotions were the net. I saw myself sailing over that net, bouncing from one side to the other.

But Meta was willing to play, and so was I, and my life went on, just like those TV daytime dramas I followed so closely, one day at a time.

Out of Sight

Claudette was panicked. Little Berry was missing. I was on-stage singing and he had gone off with his little cousin to the concession stand. His cousin came back, but without him. We were playing at Pine Knob in Michigan, an indoor/outdoor ampitheater with 5,000 screaming fans and Claudette trying to get to me, trying to tell me to stop the show, to get on the mike and make an announcement, to do something, anything, to find Berry.

She fought her way to the front, just when I was winding up the show. I was bending over the stage to shake hands with the fans when Claudette wedged herself in between the other women looking to touch me, all the while yelling, "Smokey! Smokey!"

Backstage, even after she'd found Berry, she was furious with me, and I didn't know why. Didn't know what she was talking about.

"Doo!" she yelled. "I was screaming for your attention to tell you that our son was missing. And when you came down the line and shook everyone's hand, you shook mine and said, 'Thank you very much,' and kept on going, just like I was one of your fans."

"That's 'cause I didn't even recognize you, baby!"
And that's when I knew I needed glasses.
Been wearing contacts ever since.

For a long time I'd been convinced that other Motown artists, like the Miracles, were being short-sighted. They'd left the company for what looked like greener pastures. Made me think of Motown as a university. Once we schooled them, the big cats with the big checks would be waiting by the graduation gates, talkin' 'bout, "Come with me!"

This happened in the seventies, when music was passing from the age of the producer to the age of the artist. Now, more than ever before, singers were making huge money demands. Same thing was happening with star athletes. As a company we'd done great, but our resources were nothing next to giants like Columbia, Warner Brothers and RCA. They could—and damn near did—buy any artist they wanted. Only loyalty could keep our people in the fold. Finally, just the hard-core cats remained—Stevie, me and, later on, Lionel Richie.

The Jacksons left in 1976, but that, I believe, has to do with their father, Joe. Joe never got used to Berry calling the shots on his boys. He figured because his sons came from his seed, he'd be their boss forever. Problem was that Joe wasn't a businessman. In the end he was more of a hindrance than a help; business people didn't want to deal with him. Sadly, when they were old enough, his kids found managers of their own, with Michael leading the way.

The Jacksons split-up with Motown wasn't pretty. Jermaine decided to stay with us, not because Berry was his father-in-law, but because he thought Joe was wrong. Joe demanded an audit for past royalties, but when the accountants were through, turned out he owed Motown $50,000.

Motown has been bad-mouthed in other ways. Many myths about Motowners have been perpetuated over the years. Most of them are bunk.

The first concerns my voice. Since Jump Street, I've heard critics calling me a "falsetto singer." The truth is that my range is naturally high, and, except for an occasional "ooooo" or "dooooo" left over from doo-wop days, I don't sing in falsetto.

I also tire of critics who indulge in the "death of . . ." syndrome—the death of the blues, the death of jazz, the death of soul music. Some critics confuse themselves with God, thinking that life-and-death matters are actually in their hands.

The death of the Motown sound was a big beef among writers. That sound died in the sixties, they said, and Motown along with it. But what about the movies we made or the artists, like the Jacksons or the Commodores or Rick James, we continued to develop? Besides, was Dad's *What's Going On* molded as part of the Motown sound? No; it was a synthesis of that sound but, more importantly, a harbinger of things to come.

The Motown sound was a young sound created by a bunch of young people at a certain place and time. We got older, we got married, had babies, moved away. Expecting us to keep that same sound would be like expecting us to stay nineteen forever. We evolved from a producer-oriented company into an era when artists started shaping their own individual sounds. We helped initiate that era.

There's also a general notion now—at least in some quarters—that crossover is ruining black music. After thirty years in this business, I can't help but laugh. I laugh because I was hearing this same shit thirty years ago.

When Motown first started hitting, for example, writers were calling us "white bread soul," saying that we were pandering to middle-class America by homogenizing gut-bucket black music. Well, when I listened to the shouting of the Contours or Levi Stubbs or David Ruffin or Dennis Edwards, the soul singing of Martha Reeves or Tammi Terrell, it sure as hell sounded like the real deal to me.

Jump to the seventies. I remember cats talkin' 'bout how the Golden Age of Soul was dead. By that, they meant the days of Otis Redding and Sam and Dave and Wilson Pickett were no more. But look what happened: Al Green, Teddy Pendergrass, Donny Hathaway, Bill Withers, Stevie Wonder's magnificent *Songs in the Key of Life*—all products of the seventies.

Then they called disco dipshit, yet disco produced some brilliant, bristling soul music—terrifically tough tracks by Van McCoy, Hal Davis and especially Harvey Fuqua's burning barnstormers for Sylvester. I also loved what Giorgio Moroder and Pete Bellotte did with Donna Summer.

In the eighties, I'd hear the same sad cry—rhythm and blues is dead, killed by the need to sell to white folk. Another weak-minded myth. In the eighties, Michael Jackson—a proud product of Motown—would get funkier than ever before. Prince would emerge as another super-funkster. I'm not always nuts about his lyrics, but I hear Prince's erotic dance music as dark as ancient Africa. Same goes for Terrence Trent D'Arby. Earlier in the decade, Luther Vandross would prove to be one of the great soul singers in history. These cats ain't giving up the funk, they're just changing it around.

That's the point: funk doesn't die, it develops. It was here before us and it'll be here after us. It's changed—by technology, by instrumentation—yet it hasn't changed. Dinah Washington tried to get over with the same sort of big ballads Whitney Houston is singing now. In Dinah's day, they wouldn't let her through. Some progress is being made, and Whitney's where she should be—on top. To my ears, though, she's still singing her ass off. So is Anita Baker, sounding like the new Sarah Vaughan.

Black music in America has always reached out to everyone. That's its very nature—to include, not exclude. Like the religious roots from which it springs, it's a music of gratitude and generosity. Black musicians—singers and writers and producers—have always dreamed the Tin Pan Alley dream of mainstream hits. Why not? Billie Holiday created her most powerful art—her blackest, most heartrending singing—reshaping the white pop songs of her day. When Ray Charles sang "Am I Blue?" or "Georgia," no one accused him of compromising.

I do, though, accuse the music business of a sort of racism. I hate the way the trade magazines organize the charts according to category—pop, black, etc.

To my mind, that's segregation. I'd like to see one all-encompassing chart.

After three decades of hits, I resent having to work my way to the top of the black chart before being allowed to cross over. That's like having to work your way from the back of the bus. It's bullshit.

I was thrilled when the Beatles sang my "You've Really Got a Hold on Me," when Linda Ronstadt redid "Ooo Baby Baby" and "The Tracks of My Tears," when Kim Carnes hit big with "More Love." Ironically, though, when I sang those tunes I was required to top the black chart before crossing

215

over; later, sung by whites, the same songs entered the pop charts right off the bat.

The categories need to fall.

In art, language, literature, music and religion, black Americans have a beautiful culture. Our heritage needs to be honored and studied. To a large degree, it's been our survival. But it's never simply been a matter of rejecting the white influence or the white buying public. Black artists have adapted, altered, deepened and, in many instances, discovered the future for American culture at large. That's been especially true in music. As innovators, we've led the way, not only through God-given talent, but by ingesting everything we heard around us—from cornball country waltzes to cowboy songs, my first musical love.

Cookin' and Cruisin'

Aretha opened the oven and took out the cornbread. It was piping hot. She sliced a piece and slipped in a wad of butter which melted all down the sides. Together with the baked chicken, the collard greens, and the corn on the cob, it was a meal you'd kill for.

"Baby," I told her as we sat in her kitchen in Encino, "this is making love to my stomach. You've really made me happy."

"Wish I could make myself happy, Smoke, but I just don't think L.A. life agrees with me. I miss Detroit. I miss my family and my friends."

"It's a big adjustment, I know, but this is the entertainment capital of the world."

"Smokey Robinson, what you talkin' 'bout? You know you went through this same shit with Berry about moving out here. Just 'cause you've adjusted, don't be getting on my case. I want to go home."

Two years later, after Reverend Franklin had been critically wounded in an attempted robbery in his home, she did.

*   *   *

I finally did it.

It took me five years. Marv Tarplin had given the track to me in the early seventies, and here it was, 1978, and I still couldn't think of words for the thing. Two albums had gone by—*Smokey's Family Robinson* and *Deep in My Soul*—two hitless albums, and yet, all the while, I knew I had the goods. The sales department was screaming for my new album. I had all the tunes done, except I knew the real bomb was still on Marv's demo tape. If only I could think of the words . . .

Marv's music was slow and seductive, a grinding groove with a bluesy base, loping and light and irresistible as a warm woman's smile.

Certain lyrics came to mind, but they were unconnected—". . . this is not a one-night stand, baby . . . let the music take your mind . . . just release and you will find . . . you're going fly away . . . glad you're going my way . . . inch by inch, we get closer and closer to every little part of each other."

I was getting closer to the hook, but where was it?

Then one smoggy afternoon, cruising down Sunset Strip, I was listening to the radio when they played the Young Rascals' old hit, "Groovin'."

That's it! I thought. *That's the shit I been looking for!* I loved the way the word "groovin'" sounded; it'd sing perfectly. But no, that's already been done.

That night another word practically knocked me out of bed—*cruisin'*!

Great! Absolutely perfect!

Had my hook, but still didn't have the right production.

See, I wanted it to sound kicked-back but slammin', mellow but ballsy, big and small, all at the same time.

Again, the radio gave me the clue. Driving down Santa Monica Boulevard, I happened to hear the Temps' old "Just My Imagination" when suddenly I knew I'd found the sound. Norman Whitfield produced that song with timpani drums, giving it just the open sensation I'd been searching for.

Slammed on the brakes, negotiated a quick U, and sped straight to the studio, where I called up a timpani drummer and, two hours later, had my track. The company wanted the album immediately, which meant doing my vocal in a blinding flash. Problem was that I was hoarse. I sang anyway, but to this day, I'm unhappy with my singing on "Cruisin'."

"Cruisin'," by the way, just didn't cruise up the charts. It got caught in nasty traffic along the way.

"Been listening to your new album, Smoke, and I think 'Get Ready' is the single."

"What!" I said to Berry. "Man, you're crazy!"

I'd recut "Get Ready," a sixties smash I'd written and produced on the Temps, only this time dressed up as disco. Disco was happening then. Motown had a huge hit, Thelma Houston's "Don't Leave Me This Way." Those were the glory days of Donna Summer and the Bee Gees' *Saturday Night Fever*.

"Your disco thing, Smoke," said Berry, "is cookin'. That's the track."

"What about 'Cruisin'?"

" 'Cruisin' ' is cool, but it's a throwaway, man, it's just another album cut."

I argued like hell. "Disco's fine," I said, "but I think 'Cruisin' ' is a classic. It cuts across all categories."

No use. Sales department went along with Berry. "Get

Ready" got played in the discos, but never popped on the pop charts.

Then fate took over; a disc jockey in Chicago took a fancy to "Cruisin'." Started playing it off the album, *Where There's Smoke . . .* Interest started building. Listeners started calling.

First time I heard something was happening was a week before a Chicago concert.

"Now when you get up here, Smoke," said the promoter, "you can play 'Get Ready,' but you better be ready with 'Cruisin' ' 'cause the jocks are playing that jam to death. Baby, that record's going through the roof!"

Turned out to be the first number-one single of my solo career.

Dad had been searching for a number-one single for years. Maybe that's why he dropped out of sight. His *I Want You* hit in '76, but this was '79. Marvin Gaye was hiding out in Hawaii and, I heard, coming unwound.

I worried about him, and when I landed in Honolulu for a concert date, I went to see him. He was living in a condo. The door was ajar, and I walked in, nearly tripping over the guys sleeping on the floor. The cats looked strung out.

I looked up, and there, at the top of a winding staircase, was Dad himself, in a robe, motioning me to join him.

We hadn't seen each other in a while. We hugged. I saw by his eyes that he'd been frying his brain with coke.

"I know you've come over to get on my case," he said.

"Hate to see you do yourself in, Dad."

"Got a little toot problem," he admitted, "but I can stop whenever I want."

Divorced from Anna, he'd married Janis and was on the verge of divorcing her.

"Being a sex symbol," he said, "isn't what it seems. You know that as much as me, Smoke. Women are not only willing, but dying to screw us. One nod and they come running. What man wouldn't? Who's strong enough to resist?"

"It goes with the territory," I replied, thinking of the temptations I'd both avoided and tasted.

"Well, I'm leaving the territory. I'm going to Europe, man."

"What'll that prove?"

"Give me a chance to regroup. Need to clear my head so I can start writing again. Got a whole comeback battle plan mapped out. Right now, though, my cash is a little tight. These divorce lawyers are draining me dry. Man, if you could spare $5,000 . . ."

"I don't have that kind of money on me, Dad. Besides, I'd have to think about it."

"Think about what?" he asked angrily. "In the old days you wouldn't have to think a second before loaning a friend five G's."

"Call me when I get back to L.A. Meanwhile, cool it with the coke."

"Gonna stop next week. Got this plan . . ."

A week later, Marvin called.

"Where's the money?" he wanted to know.

"Decided not to send it."

"How come, man?"

" 'Cause it'll only wind up up your nose."

"You don't know that."

"My bread isn't going to help you, Dad. It's only going to hurt."

"Okay, man, fuck it," he said before slamming down the phone.

Three years would pass before we spoke again.

*   *   *

In Marvin's madness I might have seen a preview of my own paranoia, but I wasn't looking. I was preoccupied with a change in my own affairs. It involved Meta. We were still seeing each other, but I found out she was also seeing another guy, a young actor.

Because I could never give Meta all of me, I always knew it was going to happen. But now that it was here, it still hurt. And there was no one to blame but myself.

Love Story Revisited

"You could've told me."

"But, G.E., you found out anyway."

"I know, but I would have rather heard it from you."

"I didn't want to hurt you."

Sounded like what I told Claudette when I left her, only this time it was Meta telling it to me.

I couldn't help but cry. I loved this lady. But I also had to tell the truth. "I want what's best for you," I said. "I want you to be happy. I couldn't expect you to stay with me—not when you can only have me on the run. That's not fair to you. If this cat wants you for his only woman, he's doing more than me. He's accessible to you at all times, and I'm not. You and him don't have to duck and hide. That's freedom, baby, and you deserve it."

I talked a good game, but, believe me, deep down inside, I hurt. Anyway, I cut it off. I left.

"Do you think I'm crazy to leave Motown?" Diana Ross asked.

It was 1981 and Diana's drive for independence was at its height. She'd moved to New York. From her penthouse at the Sherry Netherland she'd called me in Beverly Hills.

"I don't think it's necessarily crazy, baby," I said, "but I do think there's something to say for the people who raised you and understand you best."

"What about the money, Smoke?"

RCA had offered her a fortune.

"We'll never be able to match it. If you make the decision on bread alone, we don't have a prayer."

"But wouldn't it be good for me to get away, to start planning on my own? Don't you think I've been too pampered and protected?"

"I think you've been loved. Maybe spoiled. But look what it's done for you. This 'Endless Love' thing is your biggest single yet."

"I'm confused, Smoke, I really am. Can I come out and talk to you about it?"

"Anytime, baby, anywhere."

We carried on the dialogue in person. I tried to make Diana see that self-management wasn't easy. First Berry and then Mike Roshkind had done a phenomenal job of shepherding the Supremes and Diana's solo career into the richest possible pastures. They'd made few mistakes; Ross was now a superstar, a show-business legend. Why bite the hand that feeds you?

"If I don't try to go it alone, I'll never know," she explained.

"Whatever happens," I told her, "I'm going to be pulling for you."

Since signing with RCA she's only had one real hit, Michael Jackson's "Muscles." She calls me now and then, but I hardly hear that pushy perky energy that once characterized my neighborhood buddy. She sounds a little lost, as though she's living in an opulent world where no one knows where she comes from and no one knows who she is.

Kandi had moved to L.A. It'd been many years since we'd been together. Don't know whether it was my heartache over Meta, or whether I'd never really put Kandi out of my mind. Either way, when I went to visit my niece Sylvia and her husband, who were temporarily living with Kandi, the old fire was rekindled—not as a frequent thing, but as a once-in-a-while treat for us both. I was moved by her loyalty; even though she couldn't count on me, she had refused to see other men. I was always fascinated by her intellect as well as her sensuous beauty. I valued Kandi; I loved her.

Sometime in the early eighties I felt myself slipping away from Claudette, not into the arms of other women, but into a strange state of doubt.

No matter what happened with Meta—or, for that matter, with Kandi—Claudette remained not only a great person in my mind but a girlfriend, my first, who could never be replaced. Yet something was missing.

Early in our marriage we told each other that if one of us ever fell out of love, he or she would have to say so. We would not be one of those couples who'd stay together for forty years just so they could tell people they've been together for forty years, when, in truth, for twenty of those years they hadn't slept together. It frightened me to think about it, but slowly our romance was evaporating. For a long time I did nothing about it—I'm not good at letting go; I couldn't face the fact of leaving home again—and, as a result, I ate myself up inside.

Father Knows Best

We were in Paris. Five had gone on tour with me. A song I'd written and sung, "Being with You," had hit big and being with Daddy was always a blast. He wanted to see the Eiffel Tower and we took the elevator all the way to the top. On the way up I noticed him noticing the foxes riding with us. At eighty-six the cat was still a bull.

"Damn," he said, looking over the city covered by white puffy clouds, "these Frenchmen sure like building churches."

"Remember the church I got married in?" I asked.

"Warren Avenue Baptist Church, over by Claudette's house. Sure, I remember."

"Feels like I've been married forever."

"Boy, y'all started dating when you were babies."

"Think we started too young?"

"Thinking about that don't do no good. You got a beautiful family, ain't you?"

"Yeah, but I'm feeling fenced in."

"You've been saying that for years."

"I'm feeling it more, Daddy. More than ever."

"I never seen anyone who sweats over this stuff like you.

227

Hell, most of my partners are dead, and those who ain't don't even know how many kids they got or with which women. In my day, boy, we did what we wanted."

Man, you were lucky, but your day is gone, I wanted to say, but didn't have the heart.

Five's day wasn't gone—not yet. Wherever I traveled, he went with me. I was grateful to God for having the means to make him comfortable the last twenty-five years of his life. He was a wise and wonderful friend, a doting grandfather, a hardworking old-fashioned man who muscled his way out of Alabama to a better life in tough towns like Cleveland and Detroit.

When he was eighty-seven me and my sister gave him a birthday party. He was still going strong.

The next day, though, he was so tired he stayed in bed. I didn't think much of it, but on the second day, when he still hadn't gotten up, I knew something was wrong. Five was always up and out early, fixing lawn mowers or tuning cars.

"Hey, Daddy, you really don't look good."

"Be fine tomorrow, boy. Just lemme rest."

I let him rest, but the next day he was even weaker. I'd seen enough. I dressed him and took him to the doctor. Doc gave him a quick exam and immediately called his nurses. "Get an ambulance—and do it now. This man's going to the hospital."

"What is it?" I asked.

"He had a heart attack two days ago. It's a miracle he's alive."

Five survived the blow, but he was never the same. His energy was sapped, and he hated it.

At eighty-eight he suffered his second attack. He recovered again, but this time ended up even more discouraged. Now he was walking with a cane.

"Boy, if I have to go back in that hospital," he said, "I ain't coming out."

"Don't talk like that, Daddy. You're going to out-last us all."

"Rather be dead than half alive," he muttered.

At eighty-nine he had his third attack. From then on, he was seriously sick.

I was playing in New York when he was hospitalized with pulmonary problems. He was the one who called to tell me.

"Boy," he said in a voice shaking with pain, "when you gonna be back?"

"In a week. Why?"

"I'm in the hospital and I'm just wondering."

"I'll be home first thing tomorrow."

"Don't bother. I'll wait for you."

"What do you mean 'wait'?"

"I'll wait . . . that's all."

He hung up. The doctors assured me he was in no imminent danger. But the next night he called again.

"You say you'll be home when?" he asked.

"In six days."

"Fine. I'll wait."

"Stop talking that shit."

"Six days is fine."

From then on he called me every night while I was gone, asking the same question, assuring me he would wait.

When I finally arrived in L.A. I went straight to the hospital and brought him home. Leon Kennedy, the actor, was waiting for us.

I call Leon my brother brother. I met him at Leo's Casino in Cleveland. It was the sixties and he wasn't even old enough to get into the club. He snuck backstage. People had been telling him he looked like me and he wanted to see for himself. Once I met him, I adopted him for life. I loved him.

Over the years, he was known as Leon the Lover. In one month, he'd have more women than I'd know in a lifetime. I never imagined that one woman could ever hold him down.

"I met her, Smoke." It was five in the morning and Leon, all worked up, was on the other end of the line.

"Met who, man? And this better be good, 'cause I was dreaming of something sensational."

"The girl I'm gonna marry."

"Bullshit. I don't believe that. You, Leon the Lover, married? The folks down in hell better get themselves overcoats 'cause it's about to freeze over."

"No, man, I'm serious. Her name's Jayne Harrison. She's the former Miss Ohio and the finest, sweetest chick I've ever seen."

"When did you meet her?"

"Today. But already I know this is forever."

A year later, me and Leon were standing at the altar, waiting for Jayne as she walked down the aisle. What a beautiful bride! I was his best man, still amazed that he was actually getting married. But by then I knew Jayne Kennedy, and I knew why Leon was awestruck.

In some ways, I always felt protective of Leon. But in the final analysis, he was the one who protected me. See, Leon became a highly evolved, deeply spiritual man. He loved Five as much as me. He also knew that Daddy was a doubter.

Leon was determined to get him to accept the Lord before he died, and, by God, he did.

When we got home from the hospital, it was clear that Daddy wanted to die. He'd just been waiting to say good-bye to me. I could feel him letting go.

That last night of Daddy's life was hell. He was sweating bullets, flaying his arms, kicking his feet, looking like he was fighting off the devil. Leon went in there—calm and centered—and, miraculously, comforted him during his moment of maximum need.

I went in afterwards. He'd stopped struggling. I could see the light in his eyes. He'd surrendered. It was scary, but also beautiful. I kissed him on his lips.

"I love you," I said.

"Boy ..." he whispered, "I love you too."

He closed his eyes. He was gone.

Down

I'm no shrink.

When I've gone through hard times, I've never stopped to analyze why, never seen the need. Afterwards, though, looking back, I can see certain patterns.

I can see, for example, that losing Daddy, even though I was in my forties when it happened, affected me more than losing Mama when I was ten. Five had been such a close part of my life for so long—since the day I was born—I never figured on being without him. He was the one constant, the guy I could always count on. Because he'd beaten back sickness so many times, I believed his heart would never stop pumping. It was hard to admit it, but with him gone, I felt frightened. Without Daddy's advice, without his emotional support, I wasn't sure what would happen to me.

Claudette helped, but somehow I was feeling estranged from her. Kandi helped too. I told you how she knew and loved Daddy. It was around this same time, though, that she hit me with startling news.

"I'm pregnant," she said.

Though I'd always urged her to date, Kandi had never had any men but me. And though the doctors had always told her she could never conceive, we had obviously proven them wrong.

"If you don't want this baby," she said to me, "I'll go away and have it alone. I mean that."

"I couldn't do that. It's my baby as well as yours. We'll go through this thing together."

And we did.

I can't say I was thrilled about having a child outside of my marriage—I knew what this would do to Claudette—but it was my responsibility, my baby. Besides, like my other two children, Kandi's child would also be a miracle, created against the certainty of medical science which had claimed conception was impossible.

I knew Kandi would never have an abortion.

She said, "I want something that's part of you, angel. I want this baby."

I would never have urged her to do anything but follow her own instincts. I'm a man who believes that, in this delicate matter, it's the woman who must decide; it's her body—not the man's—that's being altered.

"I'm going to spend as much time with you during the pregnancy as I can," I promised.

I kept that promise, and in 1984 my son Trey was born. I praised God for the gift of his life. He was healthy and strong, clear-eyed and handsome. I was proud.

I'd planned to tell Claudette while Kandi was pregnant, but something got in the way—her plans for our twenty-fifth wedding anniversary.

*   *   *

Ever since Claudette and I had been married, she maintained a simple position. "Doo," she said, "I can tolerate just about anything concerning you and another woman, long as you don't put it up in my face, long as you don't disrespect me. There is, though, one thing that would make me leave you—if you ever had a baby with another woman." Those words were profound; they touched my heart because I knew they were born out of Claudette's difficulty in carrying a pregnancy till term. Lord knows she had tried so many times.

How could I—a man looking to get out of his marriage —be afraid of my wife leaving me? I don't know, but I was. Maybe I'd grown accustomed to her being my other half. Losing her would be like losing half of me. Could it be that, with or without her, I'd be a lost soul?

Claudette knew something was wrong. She knew things were coming to a head. She wanted us to remarry for our twenty-fifth anniversary. Friends we knew were celebrating the same anniversary and suggested we have a double wedding.

I thought about it. I tried to get back into my marriage, back into Claudette, but my heart wouldn't budge. My heart was somewhere out there. I'm not sure where my heart was, but I knew it wasn't at home.

"I can't do it, baby, I can't do it just for appearance's sake."

"You're so far away," Claudette said. "You're somewhere off in space."

This was when my drug thing began, when I started smoking rock cocaine cigarettes. I'd sneak the shit around the house; little by little, I'd get higher and higher.

"I want you to reconsider our remarriage," Claudette said. "It really means a lot to me."

I reconsidered. I tried. I just couldn't.

"I've had a baby with Kandi," I finally found the courage to tell her after our anniversary had passed.

Unlike the past, when she'd always weathered the storms I'd rained on her, now Claudette lost control. She cried; she screamed; she shook with anger; she told me that was it; it was all over.

This was the straw that broke the camel's back.

I said I understood. I had no explanations. It happened. I was responsible. The child was mine.

I decided to move out.

"To be with Kandi?" Claudette wanted to know.

"No. To be by myself. To figure out what I want to do. I don't expect you to wait for me. If you want to file for divorce, I'll understand. I can't say anything except that I'm sorry."

I left, found an apartment, got higher and higher, fell lower and lower.

Meanwhile, my recording career was going down the toilet. I hadn't had a hit since "Being with You," and that was four years ago. I was too fucked up to run, too fried to play golf, too frazzled to do concerts.

Berry Gordy grew alarmed.

"Come up to my place, man, I need to talk to you."

He kept me up at his Bel Air mansion for a week, trying to talk some sense into me.

"I'm not into the drug thing that much, man," I lied.

"Bullshit."

"I can stop when I want to."

"More bullshit."

All the time I was there, I was thinking about getting high, thinking I was fooling Berry, thinking I was fooling everyone. I never had any dope with me, though, out of respect for Berry and his position. What's more, he maintains a strict no-drug policy which I wasn't about to defy.

We'd walk around his grounds. He had llamas and peacocks and owls. The pool glistened with sunlight. Servants brought me mineral water and herb tea.

"Stay as long as you want, Smoke," he urged. "But just promise me you'll stop."

I promised him; I lied.

In his guesthouse, where I slept, he put magazine articles and brochures outlining the dangers of coke. I didn't care.

Daddy was dead. Trey was alive. Claudette was hurt. Kandi was worried. Kandi begged me to tell her what was happening. She knew something was wrong. But I wouldn't say a word.

The kids were missing me, I was missing myself, running from myself, smoking this shit till it made me so sick I needed more.

After six months I told Claudette to go ahead and divorce me.

"Does that mean it's all over?" she asked.

"I guess so."

"Well, I won't do it, Smokey. I won't divorce you. Despite everything, it's not a divorce I want. You're going to have to initiate the procedure. I won't."

Two days later, in a fatigued fogged-over state of mind, I went to see a lawyer.

"What are your grounds for divorce?" he asked.

"None," I said. "My wife's a wonderful woman. I love her, I'm just not *in* love with her anymore."

He said something about irreconcilable differences. I nodded. She got the papers.

She grew angry and bitter.

One day I went to see the kids and bumped into Claudette. When I tried to act civil, she was short and hostile with me.

"Why can't we still be friends?" I asked.

"Friendship and divorce don't coincide," she answered. "Statistics prove that."

"Don't talk to me about statistics," I said. "This is you and me, Boo Boo. We've cared about each other for thirty years. That doesn't have to change. I'll care about you and I hope you'll care about me for the rest of our lives."

I'd reached her. For a moment she grew warmer, came off her attitude, asked after my health. I was defensive, said I was fine, said nothing was wrong. But Claudette knew me; she knew I was lying.

"What about you, baby?" I asked.

She'd put on weight and I worried about her high blood pressure. She, too, was defensive. We were both hurting so bad, until our hearts practically burst from the pain.

This was the woman I'd loved all my life, but a woman, I knew, I'd never live with again.

The thought of that, the guilt behind it, had me up night after night. Those little cocaine cigarettes drove away the pain.

"Get me more," I told my man. "I want more."

"I want you to come to my baptism," Claudette said. "You said we were friends. Well, it's important to me that you're there."

"I'll be there," I promised.

Claudette had rediscovered religion; she'd renewed her relationship with God. I was happy, but I was also high, even at the Church on the Way, scene of the ceremony.

In a suit and tie, I sat there next to Tamla and Berry. By now they were beautiful teenagers. I felt anything but beautiful. I watched Claudette being submerged in holy water. She cried, and so did I, cried for her joy, cried for our love, cried for myself.

I left the church filled with some spirit I couldn't contain. So I got high.

I stayed high.

"People are after me, people are following me," I told my friend Forest Hairston, who'd always been there for me in times of trouble.

"You're sick, baby brother," he said. "You're hallucinating. You need help. Let me help you."

But I wouldn't let Forest, I wouldn't let anyone near me.

Relatives and close friends started weeping for me.

Promoters wondered why I wasn't working.

So I booked a concert date. Even at my lowest ebb, my fans never knew about my condition, never deserted me. I could always draw a crowd.

Before I went on, though, I got extremely fucked-up high.

Went out and faced the audience. I sang, but with none of the old fire. Instead, I saw ghosts—Jackie Wilson collapsing on stage, Sam Cooke being shot through the heart. What if my heart gave out?

"He's dead," I heard imaginary voices say as I walked back to my dressing room. "The guy's good as dead."

PART FIVE

Up

Brother Brother

In a half-awake half-asleep daydream, I remembered the last time I'd seen Marvin Gaye.

Gwen Gordy gave a birthday party for her brother Fuller.

Marvin was back from Europe on the heels of "Sexual Healing." He was triumphant.

"Told you I had a plan, man," he said, hugging me as though he'd never been mad at me.

"I'm happy for you, Dad. This is the best comeback I've ever seen."

"You ain't pissed I left Motown?"

"I'm just glad you're working again, man. Everyone's glad for you."

He was high that night, and I could feel the drugs manipulating his moods. I knew he still wasn't right.

Months passed. He went on tour and there was talk that the tour was bedlam, talk that Marvin was so coked out he was dropping his pants during the shows, talk he was acting crazy and falling deep into despair. I tried contacting him, but never got through.

Then, on April Fool's Day, 1984, the news came in. It was a cold shock, a kick in the groin. I heard it on the radio:

Dad was dead. Killed by his father.

My first thoughts were—it's a mistake, it's impossible, the news is wrong. But the news was right.

I wept. I sang and spoke at his funeral. A friend—a beautiful man—gone so early, so foolishly. I kept thinking, *the man whose seed he was took his life the day before his forty-fifth birthday.*

Now I was moving in the same direction. Why couldn't I stop myself? Why couldn't I turn it around?

My days were dark, my nights filled with fear.

Someone brought over a video tape, said it would make me feel better. *Motown 25*, one of the greatest nights of my life.

Everyone had come home for the TV special, even those who'd been bitching and moaning for years. It was the ultimate tribute to Berry Gordy, and I loved every minute of it.

Tops, Temps, Miracles, Marvelettes, Martha and Mary and Diana and Dennis and Marvin and Michael and Jermaine, "Pride and Joy" and "Jimmy Mack" and "My Guy" and "My Girl" and "Baby Love" and "Reach Out" and "Cloud Nine," every writer and every producer, everyone who'd been touched by Berry came back to say, "Thanks, man . . . thanks a lot."

Suddenly I saw the Hitsville house again, all of us together, stomping in the studio, playing ball on the lawn, poker in the back room, company picnics in cabins in the woods, Monday morning meetings, me and the Miracles on the road, Claudette snuggling up next to me . . .

Another coke-soaked cigarette, another good cry, another call to my man for another rock . . .

*   *   *

... The knock on the door was loud and persistent. At first I thought I was dreaming. Then I got scared. Maybe it was the cops, maybe a killer. Fear was all up in my face.

"Open the door, man! Open it now!"

I knew Leon Kennedy's voice. I let him in.

"Smoke," he said. "You look like shit. What the hell are you doing to yourself, man? Why do you want to die?"

"I ain't dying, just cooling out."

"Coke's got you so disgusted with yourself, you can't stop. Can't you see the vicious cycle?"

"Get off my ass, Leon. You don't know what you're talking about," I lied. Dopers always lie to cover up.

I didn't tell him about the stomach pains, the pus passing out of my body, the heart palpitations, the cold sweats.

"You look like a ghost, Smoke. Your skin's turning green, your eyes are all sunken into your head, you're wasting away to nothing."

"I don't want to talk about this anymore. I'm doing fine, man, just leave me alone."

"No, I'm not leaving at all. I'm staying here and I'm praying for you. I don't care how long it takes."

Leon stayed and prayed for me all night; he prayed till the sun came up; he wouldn't leave me; he stayed at my house all the next day and that night insisted that we go to a place called Ablaze Ministry. I called Ivory Stone, my close friend and backup singer, to come along. I'd been in contact with Ivory during these miserable months. She'd been about my only source of comfort. The few times I did eat, she was the one who fed me. When she first came to sing with me in 1975, I loved her immediately. She's a warm and wonderful person, physically gorgeous, inwardly beautiful, the kind of woman any man would be proud to call his own. She turned me on to Jesus; she's been a strong spiritual and emotional influence on my life.

Ablaze wasn't a church, just a small building in a working-class neighborhood on Florence Avenue where people were up and singing. Everyone looked joyful and glad. It wasn't an all-black hallelujah holy revival, but rather a room filled with different type people—Orientals, Chicanos, whites and blacks. The leader was a heavy-set black woman.

"That's Jean Perez," Leon whispered in my ear.

I'd never seen a woman preacher before, and she was dynamite. She didn't come at you from the bible; she came from the street, said how she'd done it all herself—the drugs and drinking—and she'd seen another way. She was real. Her speech was captivating.

"I feel the annointing coming on," she said. "The annointing is very strong in my hands. Everyone who feels like they've got arthritis, come up here now."

Five or six people got up and started walking towards her while I started thinking, *Oh shit, here comes the show. Now ain't this a bitch! Leon brought me down here to see some weird woman who's planted people in the audience to make us think she's a miracle worker.*

I stayed skeptical, even as she started healing people with arthritis, cancer and heart disease. I watched as she touched them, prayed over them and caused them to pass out from the power of her prayers.

"You," she said, pointing to me. "Would you please come up here?"

I looked around, embarrassed, hoping she meant someone else. She didn't.

Tentatively, slowly, I made my way to the podium where

she stood. She hugged me, much as a mother might hug a son. I felt the heat of her breath as she whispered into my ear away from the microphone so only I could hear.

"I know who you are," she said. "I didn't call your name because not everyone recognized you. You look so bad. I been praying for you for a year now. The Lord put you on my heart. He really loves you. You're one of His children. And He sent you here tonight so I could heal you in the name of Jesus. I know about your pus, I know about your stomach, I know about your heart palpitations and the way you sweat at night."

I was stunned. I hadn't told anyone about any of those things.

"The drugs," she said, still in a whisper, "have eaten away your stomach lining. If you hadn't come here, you would have died."

Saying that, she started praying over me. Suddenly she passed out, falling back behind the podium. Chills ran through me. I stood there stunned. They tried to revive her, tried to lift her up, but she was a big woman and it wasn't easy. When she came to, she looked at me and said, "I never pass out during prayer. You're a powerful spirit in the Lord. I want you to stay after everyone leaves."

After the service, Leon, Ivory and I followed her into a small room in the back. There she prayed on me again, holding me close to her, her eyes closed tight, her heart beating loud. Then, for the second time, she passed out.

When she came to, the woman said, "Ooo wee, your spirit is strong, Smokey! You're a positive influence on people, and your influence was about to be taken from you. But now you're all right. Now you're cool. The Lord has His arms around you."

"What does that mean?" I asked.

"You'll go on with your life and you'll be a stronger person. The Lord doesn't want you to start preaching, doesn't want you to sing only gospel music. If you do, your secular fans will drop you and the gospel fans won't take you seriously. Just be you. Doing what you do, you can get millions to come over to the Lord from all over the world. Don't push your testimony. He will let you know when to give it, and He will tell you how."

I left the Ablaze Ministry that night feeling higher than at any moment of my life, higher than I'd ever been on coke, so good and so high I felt like I was walking on air.

Since that night—it's been three years—I haven't touched or wanted any form of any drug. Just like that, the desire left me.

Being in show business, I'm always around the stuff. There have been endless opportunities to get high. Miraculously, I've not even been tempted. Miraculously, I was saved.

The Lord washed me clean.

Fork in the Road

After two years of living in a fog, being clear-minded was a beautiful blessing. I could see things that were once blurs. I saw that, despite my enormous guilt about ending my marriage, it was the righteous thing to do. Otherwise, I'd be living out the rest of my days as a hypocrite. I couldn't take that, and neither could Claudette. She deserved my honesty. And I had honestly lost that romantic love which once bound us together.

On the other hand, I told Kandi that I wasn't leaving Claudette for her. Fact is, I wasn't leaving Claudette for any woman. I was losing her to find myself.

Trey would be raised as my son. I'd spend time with him as I would with Berry and Tamla, but I wasn't interested in marriage at this point.

Claudette also saw that, once I was off drugs, I was easier to deal with and talk to. Meanwhile, she'd gotten herself back in shape—lost weight and looked terrific again. The divorce proceedings went ahead.

I discovered that, in recent years, she'd spent an enormous amount of money. That became a bone of contention.

In part it was my fault. I'd given her free rein, and she'd gone hog wild—not indulging herself, but buying for the kids, relatives, even friends in need. It wasn't showy, selfish spending, but heavy spending nonetheless. If I hadn't heeded Berry's basic tax advice thirty years earlier, I would have been in trouble. The financial phase of the divorce was tough, but I managed.

I don't think, however, that either Claudette or I managed to aid her own independence after our kids were born. We were both happy to have her as a housewife, and for a person of Claudette's intellect and skills, that wasn't enough. With twenty-twenty hindsight, I can see that she lived too much through me. No man should encourage that; no woman should allow it. I now believe that no matter how much two people love each other, they should both be prepared to survive independently.

I'm not a big believer in "could of" or "should of." Still, at the end of my marriage, it was hard to resist the regrets. Late at night, alone in my apartment, I thought of a song I'd written way back when Claudette and I were a couple of teenagers, still starry-eyed in love:

Seems like love should be easier to bear
But it's such a heavy load
Worldwide travelers you ain't been nowhere
Till you've travelled down love's road
Although I may be just a stranger
Lovers, let me warn you there's a danger
Of a fork in love's road . . .

We'd reached that fork. I was going one way, Claudette another. Yet lyrics wouldn't leave my brain, words I'd written long ago, with Claudette in mind:

I will bring you a flower from the floor of the sea
To wear in your hair
I'll do anything and everything to keep you happy
Girl, to show you I care . . .

I still meant what I'd sung; I felt it. On the deepest level I knew that Claudette and I would always be together and, I was sure, Claudette knew it too.

Change Gonna Come

Berry and I were sitting in his den in his Bel Air estate, the same room where, years before, we had our nasty run-in.

I'd just gotten through telling him about the Ablaze Ministry, and his face was lit up with a smile big enough to frame.

"Man, that's terrific. And now I got some news for your ass. We're going into a whole new program with you. Your life's going to turn around, Smoke, and it's going to turn around in a hurry."

"I need a hit," I admitted.

"You need more than a hit, you need a manager. And I'm giving you the best—Mike Roshkind."

I'd known Mike for years. Since the sixties he'd been Berry's main adviser. I always saw him as a hard-core cat, but I was wrong. He turned out to be all heart. Devoted himself to my career—and the challenge of turning it around—as though it were a matter of life and death. Mike loves challenges; he's a doer, and what he did to my professional life was nothing short of remarkable.

Within thirty-six months he had me making more money than I'd ever made before, playing prestige venues around the world.

Berry helped. He came in as executive producer of my 1987 album, *One Heartbeat*. It was a little like the old days, with him critiquing and pushing me to my limits. Berry will never change. Even during my most recent tour, he didn't leave my Las Vegas show before redoing the light show and sound mix.

The album hit big, spawning three hits—"Just to See Her," "One Heartbeat" and "Love Don't Give No Reason." Making matters sweeter, the English group ABC released a tribute to me called "When Smokey Sings," a smash during the identical period as "Just to See Her." I understand that was a historical first—the tributor and the tributee going top ten at the same time.

At the 1987 Grammys, after a lifetime in show business, I won my first ever. It was for singing "Just to See Her," and it felt great.

Felt even better when, that same year, Hall and Oates introduced me as an inductee into the Rock 'n' Roll Hall of Fame. That night, at the banquet at the Waldorf Astoria in New York City, was especially trippy. I was sitting at a table with lifelong friend Cecil Franklin who was representing Aretha.

See, I got in the same time as four of my musical idols —Jackie Wilson, Clyde McPhatter, my brother Marvin Gaye and sister Aretha. I felt them clinging so close to my heart. When I went up to accept the award, they were next to me; I felt their musical spirit, felt my gratitude was their gratitude. Thinking of my heroes, I was choked up enough, but as I stepped to the podium, the audience, made up of record industry artists and execs—a tough-nosed crowd—rose to their feet, applauding and then spontaneously singing my song, "Ooo oooo ooooooooo . . . baby baby . . . ooo oooo ooooooooo . . . baby baby." I couldn't stop the tears.

God's blessings are bountiful.

Currently, I've also assembled the finest band of my career. Directed by Sonny Burke, there's David Ii on sax, Chris Ho on keyboards, Larry Ball on bass, Tony Lewis on drums, Robert "Boogie" Bowles on guitar, Ivory Stone and Pat Henley background vocals, and, the mainstay for most of my musical life, Marv Tarplin. My tour manager, Earl Bryant, is by far the best I've ever had.

In the midst of my comeback, though, something else was happening that excited rumors of all sorts. The papers were saying that Motown was being sold. And the papers proved to be right.

What's wrong, though, are reports claiming that we Motowners are depressed and distraught that Berry sold his record company to MCA.

I'm happy about it, and I'll tell you why:

I love Berry, and I love the notion that he's got a shot at some peace and quiet—to make a movie, write a book or, if he wants to, sit on a desert island and eat pineapples all day. He's earned the right.

On one hand, I'm sorry that Motown didn't survive the Age of the International Entertainment Conglomerates. Like a lot of other smaller fish, we got swallowed by a bigger whale—or really a bunch of bigger whales, those labels who'd been picking off our talent for years. It was only fair. Capitalists live and die by the sword. I ain't complaining. I'm proud of what Motown did and stands for. Berry proved a black-run firm could get to the top of one of the most cut-throat fields in American business.

Mistakes were made. Sometimes wrong executives were put in charge of wrong departments. And during his moviemaking years, Berry moved away from record concerns. Undoubtedly, that hurt.

Increasingly, though, the music business became more brutal and complex in the late seventies and eighties. Berry's frustrations grew. For years, I'd urged him to back off—I didn't want him to become one of those ulcer-eaten executives—but it wasn't until he sold the thing that he was able to breathe a sigh of relief.

I love Motown, but I love Berry more. Moreover, the sale only involved the record company. Now Motown has developed into a full-fledged enterprise, and Berry still has Jobete, his music publishing arm, as well as his movie division. Besides, MCA just signed Diana, and, after all this time, I'm looking forward to being her label-mate again.

Artistically, I feel especially confident and strong these days. I'm bubbling over with enthusiasm. I'd love to do a musical. I'd also love to go back and interpret some of those gorgeous songs—by Gershwin and Porter and Kern and Berlin—that I heard Sarah Vaughan singing when I was still a child. They sound even lovelier to me now. I have a feeling I can bring to those ballads a certain hard-earned wisdom about affairs of the heart; I want to offer those songs even more respect, more love.

The Future Is Love

Back to the Future is my favorite movie. I've seen it twenty times; I've memorized every line. The story strikes a deep chord in me, I suppose, because of how I cherish my past. My childhood chums remain close to me. I have a forty-year club with friends from the old neighborhood. I see the cats often. They keep me rooted right. They remind me where I began and who I am.

I try to stay simple. I could ego-trip about my big concert dates, but all I have to do is look over at Michael Jackson's tour to put myself back in line. Yet even Michael—who's as powerful and polished a performer as ever lived—didn't begin nor will he end show business. We're all just players, sidemen in a big show that has no end. I think of myself as a guy with a good voice and a knack for songwriting who's had some big breaks and blessings.

I drive my own car and wash out my own socks after the gig. If I meet fans on the street, I'm glad they recognize me. I'm glad they want my autograph. I've got all the time in the world for them. I don't forget that they got me here, made my life comfortable, allowed me to sing.

257

How could I not feel blessed?

When I was a kid I woke up singing. Never wanted to do anything else. Now I get to travel around the world doing what I'd do for free, only getting paid good money.

Thank you, Lord.

My relationship with Jesus comforts me when nothing else can. I feel so safe and strong and confident knowing that He's with me every minute of my life. His love is unconditional and nonjudgmental. He loves for the sake of love. My prayer is that through me His love may touch others.

In the human realm, Daddy Five remains my main man. Until his heart attacks, he was out there attacking the world. Pops Gordy was the same. They amputated his leg, but the year after, he was dancing up a storm. I like a fighter, a cat who bites down on the bone of life and won't let go till the end.

Right now, after a lifetime of excruciatingly deep romantic relationships, I'm going to take a little time to live alone, to meditate, to get to know myself.

Judgment Day

I'm sitting on the witness stand. I'm wearing my best blue suit, my best red silk tie. The judge leans forward in his high-back chair. The jurors are studying my face, anxious to hear my responses. Cameramen and reporters are standing in the back, taking notes.

I look out into the courtroom and there among the spectators, on the first row, I see three women seated next to one another: Claudette, Kandi and Meta. Each, in her own way, is dazzlingly beautiful. Each looks at me knowingly. God knows I've been intimate—physically and spiritually intimate—with all three. Seeing them together excites and confuses me.

Claudette rises. She's wearing an elegant tan tailored suit and broad-brimmed hat. Her smile is radiant.

She walks to where I'm seated.

"How do you plead, Smokey Robinson?"

"Guilty of loving you," is the only answer I can manage.

Claudette returns to her seat. Now Kandi rises. Her tight-fitting dress is a distraction. Her manner is all business. She stands before me and asks the same question.

"How do you plead, Smokey Robinson?"

What can I say? "I'm guilty of loving you."

Meta replaces Kandi. She's young and vibrant and filled with enthusiasm.

"Tell me," she says, inches from my face, "how do you plead?"

"Guilty, guilty of loving you."

The jury buzzes, the courtroom's awash with whispers. I look for my attorney, my father, my mother, my sisters, friends Berry, Leon and Forest, Cecil and Ollie, but they're nowhere in sight.

"Do you have anything to say for yourself, Mr. Robinson?" the stern-voiced judge wants to know.

I struggle to organize my thoughts, but words won't come. Only silence. Everyone's waiting on me. I take a deep breath and finally am able to say something. "Love," I say, "is so amazing that sometimes it's blinding, sometimes it's baffling, the way it helps and hurts and heals, all at the same time."

"Do you believe in free love, Mr. Robinson?" the judge asks.

"Nothing is free," I answer, "but I know that righteous love is real."

I stop talking and start singing a song which, until this moment, I've never heard before:

Love wakes you in the morning
And cushions you at night

Love makes you feel and see
A bright and wondrous light

Love's the magician
Who works the trick

Love's the miracle
That makes us tick

The courtroom turns into a concert hall; the jury, judge and spectators are now an audience of music lovers, swaying to my new song.

I wake up relieved, refreshed.

My dream is over; my new life has begun.

RECORDS

Except for his first four singles in 1957–1958—two on End Records—"Got a Job"/"Mama Done Tole Me" and "Money"/ "I Cry"—and two on Chess—"Bad Girl"/"I Love Your Baby" and "I Need a Change"/ "All I Want Is You"—Smokey Robinson's entire recorded work has been done for Motown, mainly on the Tamla label.

Reference was made to the excellent discography in *The Motown Story* (Charles Scribner's Sons, 1985).

Singles are in quotes; album titles italicized.

RON AND BILL
  Ronnie White and Smokey Robinson

    1959:   "It"/
               "Don't Say Goodbye"

THE MIRACLES

    1959:   "Bad Girl"/
               "I Love Your Baby"*

---

*Chess was national distributor.

"You Can Depend On Me"/
"The Feeling Is So Fine"

"You Can Depend On Me"/
"Way Over There"

1960: "Shop Around"/
       "Who's Loving You"

1961: *Hi! We're the Miracles!*

       "Ain't It Baby"/
       "The Only One I Love"

       "Mighty Good Lovin' "/
       "Broken Hearted"

       "Everybody's Gotta Pay Some Dues"/
       "I Can't Believe"

       "What's So Good about Goodbye"/
       "I've Been Good to You"

1962: *Cookin' with the Miracles*

       I'll Try Something New

       "I'll Try Something New"/
       "You Never Miss a Good Thing"

       "Way Over There"/
       "If Only Your Mother Knew"

       "You've Really Got a Hold on Me"/
       "Happy Landing"

1963: *Christmas with the Miracles*

       Recorded Live On Stage

*You've Really Got a Hold On Me—The Fabulous
    Miracles*

Doin' Mickey's Monkey

"A Love She Can Count On"/
"I Can Take a Hint"

"Mickey's Monkey"/
"Whatever Makes You Happy"

"I Gotta Dance to Keep from Cryin' "/
"Such Is Love, Such Is Life"

1964: *The Greatest Hits, from the Beginning—2 LPs*

Gemini

"(You Can't Let the Boy Overpower) the Man in
    You"/
"Heartbreak Road"

"I Like It Like That"/
"You're So Fine and Sweet"

"That's What Love Is Made Of"/
"Would I Love You"

SMOKEY ROBINSON AND THE MIRACLES

1965: *Going to a Go Go*

"Ooo Baby Baby"/
"All That's Good"

"The Tracks of My Tears"/
"A Fork in the Road"

"My Girl Has Gone"/
"Since You Won My Heart"

"Going to a Go Go"/
"Choosey Beggar"

1966:   *Away We Go Go*

"Whole Lot of Shakin' in My Heart"/
"Oh Be My Love"

"Come 'Round Here, I'm the One You Need"/
"Save Me"

1967:   *The Tears of a Clown*
        (original title: *Make It Happen*)

"The Love I Saw in You Was Just a Mirage"/
"Come Spy with Me"

"More Love"/
"Swept for You Baby"

"I Second That Emotion"/
"You Must Be Love"

1968:   *Greatest Hits, Volume Two*

        Special Occasion

"If You Can Want"/
"When the Words from Your Heart Get Caught Up
   in Your Throat"

"Yester Love"/
"Much Better Off"

"Special Occasion"/
"Give Her Up"

"Baby Baby Don't Cry"/
"Your Mother's Only Daughter"

1969:   *Live!*

Time Out for Smokey Robinson and the Miracles

Four in Blue

"Doggone Right"/
"Here I Go Again"

"Abraham, Martin and John"/
"Much Better Off"

"Point It Out"/
"Darling Dear"

1970:   *What Love Has Joined Together*

Pocketful of Miracles

The Season for Miracles

"Who's Gonna Take the Blame"/
"I Gotta Thing for You"

"The Tears of a Clown"/
"Promise Me"

1971:   *One Dozen Roses*

"I Don't Blame You at All"/
"That Girl"

"Crazy About the La La La"/
"Oh Baby Baby I Love You"

"Satisfaction"/
"Flower Girl"

1972: *Flying High Together*

1957–1972—2 LPs

"We've Come Too Far to End It Now"/
"When Sundown Comes"

"I Can't Stand to See You Cry"/
"With Your Love Came"

SMOKEY ROBINSON—SOLO

1973: *Smokey*

"Sweet Harmony"/
"Wanna Know My Mind"

"Baby Come Close"/
"A Silent Partner in a Three-Way Love Affair"

1974: *Anthology—Smokey Robinson and the Miracles—*
3 LPs

Pure Smokey

"It's Her Turn to Live"/
"Just My Soul Responding"

"Virgin Man"/
"Fulfill Your Need"

"I Am I Am"/
"The Family Song"

1975: *A Quiet Storm*

"Baby That's Backatcha"/
"Just Passing Through"

"Agony and Ecstasy"/
"Wedding Song"

"Quiet Storm"/
"Asleep on My Love"

1976: *Smokey's Family Robinson*

"When You Came"/
"Coincidentally"

"An Old-Fashioned Man," from the film, *Norman
    ... Is That You?*/
"Just Passing Through"

1977: *Deep in My Soul*

Big Time, movie sound track

"There Will Come a Day (I'm Gonna Happen to
    You)"/
"The Humming Song (Lost for Words)"

"Vitamin U"/
"Holly"

"Theme from 'Big Time' "—parts 1 & 2

1978: *Love Breeze*

Smokin'—Live 2 LPs

"Daylight and Darkness"/
"Why You Wanna See My Bad Side"

"Shoe Soul"/
"I'm Loving You Softly"

1979: *Where There's Smoke*

"Get Ready"/
"Ever Had a Dream"

"Cruisin' "/
"Ever Had a Dream"

1980: *Warm Thoughts*

"Let Me Be the Clock"/
"Travelin' Through"

"Heavy on Pride (Light on Love)"/
"I Love the Nearness of You"

"Wine Women and Song"/
"I Want to be Your Love"

1981: *Being With You*

Superstar Series, Volume 18, hits compilation

"Being with You"/
"What's in Your Life for Me"

"Aqui Con Tigo"
(Spanish version of "Being with You")

"You Are Forever"/
"I Hear the Children Singing"

"Who's Sad"/
"Food for Thought"

1982: *Yes It's You Lady*

"Tell Me Tomorrow"—parts 1 & 2

"Old Fashioned Love"/
"Destiny"

"Yes It's You Lady"/
"Are You Still Here"

1983: *Touch the Sky*

Blame It on Love and All the Great Hits

"I've Made Love to You a Thousand Times"/
"Into Each Rain Some Life Must Fall"

"Touch the Sky"
"All My Life's a Lie"

with Barbara Mitchell:
"Blame It on Love"/
"Even Tho"

"Don't Play Another Love Song"/
"Wouldn't You Like to Know"

duet with Rick James:
"Ebony Eyes"/
"You, Her and Me"

1984: *Essar*

"And I Don't Love You"/
"Dynamite"

"I Can't Find"/
"Gimme What You Want"

1985: *Smoke Signals*

"Hold on to Your Love"/
"Train of Thought"

"Sleepless Nights"/
"Close Encounters of the First Kind"

"First Time on a Ferris Wheel"   duet with Syreeta
from movie *The
Last Dragon*

1987: *One Heartbeat*

"Just to See Her"/
"I'm Gonna Love You Like There's No Tomorrow"

"One Heartbeat"/
"Love Will Set You Free"

"What's Too Much"/
"I've Made Love to You a Thousand Times"

"Love Don't Give No Reason"
"Hanging On by a Thread"/

"Keep Me"

"You're My Hero"   duet with Dionne Warwick on
her *Reservations for Two*
Arista album

"I Know You By Heart"   duet with Dolly Parton
on her *Rainbow* CBS
album

SELECTED SONGS OF SMOKEY ROBINSON

Of the some four thousand tunes written or cowritten by Smokey, these are his most prominent.

The songs are organized around the artists who recorded them.

THE MIRACLES

Got a Job
Bad Girl
Way Over There
You Can Depend on Me
Shop Around
Who's Loving You
What's So Good about Goodbye
I'll Try Something New
I've Been Good to You
You Really Got a Hold on Me
A Love She Can Count On
I Like It Like That
That's What Love Is Made Of
Come on Do the Jerk

Ooo Baby Baby
The Tracks of My Tears
My Girl Has Gone
Choosey Beggar
Going to a Go Go
Save Me
The Love I Saw in You Was Just a Mirage
More Love
I Second That Emotion
If You Can Want
Yester Love
Special Occasion
Baby Baby Don't Cry
Here I Go Again
Point It Out
The Tears of a Clown
I Don't Blame You at All
Satisfaction
Heart Like Mine
Won't You Take Me Back
Cause I Love You
Your Love
After All
Don't Leave Me
The Groovy Thing
You Must Be Love
Dancing Alright
The Soulful Shack
Don't Think It's Me
Once I Get to Know You
The Composer
I'll Take You Any Way That You Can
Doggone Right

The Hurt Is Over
You Neglect Me
In Case You Need Love
Since You Won My Heart
From Head to Toe
All That's Good
Let Me Have Some
A Fork in the Road
When Sundown Comes
No Wonder Love's a Wonder
Oh Baby Baby I Love You
Flower Girl
You've Got the Love I Need
Point It Out
Backfire
Swept for You Baby
More More More of Your Love
Oh Be My Love
He Don't Care about Me
If Your Mother Only Knew
This I Swear, I Promise
Your Mother's Only Daughter
Much Better Off
You Only Build Me Up to Tear Me Down
Give Her Up
That's the Way I Feel
Everybody's Gotta Pay Some Dues
Mama
Ain't It Baby
Determination
You Never Miss a Good Thing
The Only One I Love
Broken Hearted

I Can't Believe
When Nobody Cares
Dreams Dream
A Legend in Its Own Time

MARY WELLS

The One Who Really Loves You
Two Lovers
Laughing Boy
Operator
You Beat Me to the Punch
He's the One I Love
My Guy
How? When My Heart Belongs to You
When I'm Gone
I'll Be Available
Your Old Stand-By
What's Easy for Two Is Hard for One
What Love Has Joined Together

MARVELETTES

I Apologize
I Think I Can Change You
The Day You Take One (You Have to Take the Other)
The Hunter Gets Captured by the Game
You're the One
My Baby Must Be a Magician
Here I Am Baby
You're the One for Me, Baby
Don't Mess with Bill

You're My Remedy
As Long as I Know He's Mine
Marionette
A Breath Taking Guy
He's A Good Guy
Our Lips Just Seem to Rhyme Everytime
Fading Away
Take Me Where You Go
I'll Be in Trouble

THE TEMPTATIONS

The Way You Do the Things You Do
I'll Be in Trouble
My Girl
It's Growing
Since I Lost My Baby
My Baby
Don't Look Back
Get Ready
Slow Down Heart
I Want a Love I Can See
The Further You Look, the Less You See
Christmas Everyday
Baby Baby I Need You
You'll Lose a Precious Love
You're the One I Need
Fading Away
Who You Gonna Run To
You're Not an Ordinary Girl
Not Now I'll Tell You Later
No More Water in the Well
Now That You've Won Me

Don't Send Me Away
Cindy
Fan the Flame
Backstage
More on the Inside

MARVIN GAYE

I Want You Around (with Kim Weston)
Now That You've Won Me
It's a Bitter Pill to Swallow
More Than a Heart Can Stand
I'll Be Doggone
One More Heartache
Ain't That Peculiar
Symphony

FOUR TOPS

Then
Opportunity Knocks for Me
Nothing
Wonderful Baby
Is There Anything That I Can Do
Still Water
Love Is the Answer

MARTHA AND THE VANDELLAS

Keep It Up
No More Tear-Stained Make Up
Give Him Up

ISLEY BROTHERS

It's Out of the Question
Little Miss Sweetness

CONTOURS

First I Look at the Purse
This Old Miner
Whole Lotta Woman

THE SUPREMES

Your Heart Belongs to Me
You Bring Back Memories
You're My Sunny Boy
Long Gone Lover
Loving You Is Better Than Ever
Till Johnny Comes
Misery Makes Its Home in My Heart
The Loving Country
Your Wonderful Sweet Sweet Love
Floy Joy
Over and Over
Precious Little Things
Now the Bitter Now the Sweet
Automatically Sunshine
The Wisdom of Time

DIONNE WARWICK

You're My Hero

ARETHA FRANKLIN

Just My Daydream

SMOKEY ROBINSON

Sweet Harmony
Baby Come Close
What's in Your Life for Me
Ever Had a Dream
I Want to Be Your Love
Share It
Cruisin'
It's a Good Night
I Love the Nearness of You
Hanging On by a Thread
Why You Wanna See My Bad Side
Love So Fine
Shoe Soul
Trying It Again
Daylight and Darkness
Here I Go Again
Madame X
Blame It on Love
Being with You
Holly
Happy
A Silent Partner in a Three-Way Love Affair
Just My Soul Responding
Wanna Know My Mind
The Family Song
Touch the Sky
Gimme What You Want

Gone Again
All My Life's a Lie
Dynamite
I've Made Love to You a Thousand Times
Quiet Storm
The Agony and the Ecstasy
Wedding Song
Baby That's Backatcha
Love Letters
Coincidentally
When You Came
Get Out of Town
Do Like I Do
Open
So in Love
Like Nobody Can
Castles Made of Sand
It's Her Turn to Live
The Love Between Me and My Kids
I Am I Am
Asleep on My Love
Virgin Man
She's Only a Baby Herself
Fulfill Your Need
A Tattoo
Yes It's You Lady
Are You Still Here
International Baby
Let Me Be the Clock
Heavy on Pride
Into Each Rain Some Life Must Fall
Wine Women and Song
Melody Man

Theme from *Big Time*
J J's Theme
Hip Trip
He Is the Light of the World
So Nice to Be with You
Shana's Theme
If We're Gonna Act Like Lovers
Close Encounters of the First Kind
Little Girl Little Girl
Girl I'm Standing There
And I Don't Love You
Train of Thought
I Can't Find
Because of You (It's the Best It's Ever Been)
Be Kind to the Growing Mind
Te Quiero Como Si No Hubiera Un Mañana (I'm
   Going to Love You Like There's No Tomorrow)
Hold On to Your Love
It's Time to Stop Shopping Around
Why Do Happy Memories Hurt So Bad
What's Too Much
You Don't Know What It's Like
Love Brought Us Here Tonight
Love Don't Give No Reason
Keep Me

INDEX